Cambridge Elements

Elements in the Gothic
edited by
Dale Townshend
Manchester Metropolitan University
Angela Wright
University of Sheffield

BIOGRAPHY AND THE TRADE-GOTHIC AUTHOR

The Case of Isabella Kelly

Yael Shapira
Bar-Ilan University

CAMBRIDGE
UNIVERSITY PRESS

Shaftesbury Road, Cambridge CB2 8EA, United Kingdom

One Liberty Plaza, 20th Floor, New York, NY 10006, USA

477 Williamstown Road, Port Melbourne, VIC 3207, Australia

314–321, 3rd Floor, Plot 3, Splendor Forum, Jasola District Centre, New Delhi – 110025, India

103 Penang Road, #05–06/07, Visioncrest Commercial, Singapore 238467

Cambridge University Press is part of Cambridge University Press & Assessment, a department of the University of Cambridge.

We share the University's mission to contribute to society through the pursuit of education, learning and research at the highest international levels of excellence.

www.cambridge.org
Information on this title: www.cambridge.org/9781009548236

DOI: 10.1017/9781009435215

© Yael Shapira 2025

This publication is in copyright. Subject to statutory exception and to the provisions of relevant collective licensing agreements, no reproduction of any part may take place without the written permission of Cambridge University Press & Assessment.

When citing this work, please include a reference to the DOI 10.1017/9781009435215

First published 2025

A catalogue record for this publication is available from the British Library

ISBN 978-1-009-54823-6 Hardback
ISBN 978-1-009-43519-2 Paperback
ISSN 2634-8721 (online)
ISSN 2634-8713 (print)

Cambridge University Press & Assessment has no responsibility for the persistence or accuracy of URLs for external or third-party internet websites referred to in this publication and does not guarantee that any content on such websites is, or will remain, accurate or appropriate.

For EU product safety concerns, contact us at Calle de José Abascal, 56, 1°, 28003 Madrid, Spain, or email eugpsr@cambridge.org

Biography and the Trade-Gothic Author

The Case of Isabella Kelly

Elements in the Gothic

DOI: 10.1017/9781009435215
First published online: October 2025

Yael Shapira
Bar-Ilan University
Author for correspondence: Yael Shapira, shapira.yael@biu.ac.il

Abstract: This Element makes a case for the value of biography in studying Gothic novels published by trade presses during the Romantic period. As Section 1 demonstrates, biography has long played a central role in the study of canonical Gothic and in shaping the Gothic canon. In contrast, the biographical obscurity of trade-Gothic authors has contributed to the enduring marginality of their work. Using Isabella Kelly (c. 1759–1857) as a case study, the following sections demonstrate how biographical knowledge complicates our view of trade-Gothic fiction and its relation to the canon. Section 2 uses new archival findings to update Kelly's biography, while Section 3 traces covert pieces of life writing embedded in her novels. Section 4 revisits Kelly's acquaintance with Matthew Lewis, using her fiction to shed new light on their relationship and to question long-held beliefs about the flow of influence in the Gothic literary marketplace.

Keywords: Trade Gothic, Isabella Kelly, Minerva Press, Biography, Authorship

© Yael Shapira 2025
ISBNs: 9781009548236 (HB), 9781009435192 (PB), 9781009435215 (OC)
ISSNs: 2634-8721 (online), 2634-8713 (print)

Contents

1 Gothic Fiction, Biography, and the Canon/Trade Divide   1

2 Isabella Kelly's Cover Stories   15

3 Telling Truth in Fiction: *Madeline* (1794)   31

4 Kelly and Lewis: The Prequel   44

   References   61

1 Gothic Fiction, Biography, and the Canon/Trade Divide

> I must again express gratitude for these fruits of yr research concerning our mutual acquaintance Isabella Kelly. . . . The whole Kelly complex is like a game of chess in which every new move multiplies the possibilities and sends the mind speculating in every direction.
>
> (Peck, 1955b)

The lines above were written in October 1955 by Louis F. Peck, a professor at Pennsylvania State University, to Frank Algar, a British scholar and book collector. Peck was working on what would become his 1961 biography of Matthew Gregory Lewis (1775–1818), author of *The Monk* (1796), and he first contacted Algar in September 1955 to ask for any information he might have about 'Mrs. Isabella Kelly, mother of William Martin Kelly, a boy whom Lewis sponsored' (Peck, 1955a). He was interested in William because of Montague Summers' 1938 book *The Gothic Quest*, which had declared Lewis a homosexual and identified William Kelly as 'the absorbing passion of his life' (Summers, 1964: 263). In their ensuing exchange, Peck and Algar both dismissed Summers' claim as unfounded, but Peck was still eager for information about William's mother, Isabella, who received financial and professional help from Lewis. Who exactly was her first husband? Did she have two sons, or three? Wasn't there a rumour – ridiculous, surely – that they were Lewis' illegitimate children? And what else did Algar know about Lewis' connection to the Kellys – 'an interesting byway in literary history', as he put it, 'which deserves to be accurately treated if it is to be mentioned at all'? (Peck, 1955a).

It was not until the seventh letter in Peck and Algar's exchange that Algar brought in a source he had apparently not thought to consult before: Isabella Kelly's own writing. As both men knew, Kelly (c. 1759–1857) was not just the mother of Lewis' alleged love interest but the author of numerous popular novels, a poetry collection and several other works. Her writing, Algar reported, indeed contained some helpful hints about her family history (Algar, 1955b). Peck was again delighted, especially since Algar's discovery prompted one of his own: 'Yr mention of her Collection of Poems & Fables . . . served to remind me that I own a copy of the book – in fact, it was within arm's reach when I opened yr letter' (Peck, 1955b).

That two painstaking scholars should have ignored the literary output of the woman whose life they were researching – including a book that, as Peck realized, was literally at his fingertips the whole time – is not as surprising as it may sound. Much as Peck and Algar seem to have enjoyed their sleuthing, Lewis was the real focus of Peck's work. Neither man was particularly motivated to gain an in-depth understanding of Isabella Kelly, much less delve into her many volumes of writing. The woman who emerges from their correspondence is therefore a threadbare figure, a connect-the-dots outline of life events and family connections – in sharp contrast to Peck's meticulous and informed portrait of Lewis.

Peck's and Algar's vastly different levels of interest in Lewis and Kelly correspond to a broader delineation that has long shaped the study of Romantic-era Gothic fiction. Whereas Lewis has been recognized for decades as one of the major Gothic novelists of his day, Kelly belongs to a group of writers who have traditionally attracted little scholarly attention. Kelly was a regular contributor to William Lane's Minerva Press, the foremost purveyor of new novels in Romantic-era Britain and the publishing house most strongly associated with the proliferation of Gothic fiction. Already in their own day, writers of Kelly's publishing profile were dismissed as untalented hacks, and modern scholars have largely followed suit. To borrow Franz J. Potter's useful terminology, the modern study of Romantic-era Gothic has persistently cordoned off 'trade Gothic' – that is, fiction published by high-volume, low-prestige trade presses like Minerva – from the far smaller canon of celebrated fiction that Potter designates 'art-Gothic' (Potter, 2005: 2).[1]

Over time, there have been some additions to what Frederick S. Frank called 'the official circle of critically acceptable Goths created by literary historians' (Frank, 1987: xiv) – namely, Horace Walpole, Clara Reeve, Sophia Lee, William Beckford, Ann Radcliffe, Matthew Lewis, Charles Robert Maturin and Mary Shelley. Nevertheless, the work of this small group of authors is still the predictable core of most Gothic scholarship. Meanwhile, the great mass of the period's Gothic fiction, written by trade novelists such as Kelly, Anna Maria Bennett, Elizabeth Bonhôte, T. J. Horsley Curties, Francis Lathom, Anna Maria Mackenzie, Elizabeth Meeke, Eliza Parsons, Regina Maria Roche, Eleanor Sleath and others, has remained until recently little known and barely discussed.

The sharp delineation of 'canon' from 'trade' is rooted in the cultural dynamics of the Romantic period itself. As E. J. Clery has argued, the distinction between 'high' and 'popular' literature was not yet clearly in place during the novel-publishing surge of the 1790s (1995: 135–140); nevertheless, the processes that would eventually form the high/low divide were already in evidence, especially in the critical treatment of the Minerva Press. In the early 1790s, as Megan Peiser shows, the *Critical Review* and the *Monthly Review* began systematically to treat Minerva's offerings as 'a class apart from other

---

[1] Potter's category of 'trade Gothic' also includes shorter forms of Gothic storytelling, such as bluebooks, chapbooks and magazine tales, which fall outside the purview of this Element.

novels', relegating them to the Monthly Catalogue in the back pages of the periodical, where they received 'short sentences of recognition and ... sharp criticism' (Peiser, 2020: 130, 127). From the mid 1790s on, the *Monthly Review* began to ignore Minerva titles (Gamer, 2015: 540).

This bifurcation of the literary field was echoed in the critical reception of Gothic romances, whose proliferation during the 1790s was strongly associated with Lane's commercial enterprise. Responding to Radcliffe's growing success and celebrity and to the popularity (and notoriety) of Lewis' *The Monk*, reviewers quickly fell into the habit of drawing a distinction between Radcliffe and Lewis, on the one hand, and the many lesser-known authors of the trade presses, on the other. The persistent references to Radcliffe's many 'imitators' suggested that Radcliffe herself existed in a cultural sphere of her own, a status that Sir Walter Scott memorably summed up in 1824 when he declared Radcliffe one of 'the favoured few, who have been distinguished as the founders of a class, or school' (Scott, 1824: xvii). Though Samuel Taylor Coleridge found plenty to fault in *The Monk*, he nonetheless opened his 1797 review of Lewis' book by asserting its superiority: 'cheaply as we estimate romances in general', he wrote, 'we acknowledge, in the work before us, the offspring of no common genius'. Noting Lewis' singular abilities alongside his excesses, Coleridge placed the author of *The Monk* at a significant remove from the 'multitude of...manufacturers' who, he claimed, produced the many romances of the day with 'little expense of thought or imagination' (1797: 194). Modern Gothic scholarship would later reprise and strengthen this split, rescuing the canonical Gothic works from many decades of disdain by declaring them fundamentally unlike the imitative 'trash' of the trade presses. As I discuss further below (see Section 1.4), the division of Romantic-era Gothic into 'art' and 'trade' – two essentially distinct categories of literature, supposedly requiring altogether different critical practices – was foundational to the emergence of modern Gothic studies as an accepted academic discipline.

The main reason for the dismissal of trade-Gothic novels has been the continued judgement, already expressed by their contemporaries, that they are 'imitations' of more famous works, primarily those by Radcliffe and Lewis. Canonical Gothic fiction itself borrows heavily from various precursors, among them graveyard poetry, Romantic poetry, sentimental fiction, Shakespearean drama and the German *schauerroman*. But trade-Gothic novels have not been regarded as taking part in the same intertextual play and have instead been largely dismissed as what one early scholar of Gothic called an 'unappetizing gallimaufry of earlier stories' (Birkhead, 1921: 73). The growing scholarly understanding of the business strategies used by publishers like Lane, who solicited novels modelled after successful precedents in order to offer readers a 'new twist on a known pleasure' (Jacobs, 2000: 172), has only strengthened the impression of trade-Gothic fictions as being first and foremost commodities, of little interest from an artistic point of view.

This enduring critical consensus about trade Gothic has gradually changed over the last two decades or so, as more and more neglected fictions have received close, curious attention. A surge of research has advanced not only a new familiarity with forgotten novels but a new understanding of the aesthetic possibilities that exist within formulaic writing (see H. Hudson, 2020, 2023; K. Hudson, 2020; McLeod, 1997; Neiman, 2019; Neiman and Morin, 2020). While not denying that trade novels made prominent use of tropes identified with canonical writers, scholars have demonstrated that such shared materials could be used in self-aware, meaningful ways, thus challenging the term 'imitation' as an insufficient descriptor for diverse practices of appropriation and adaption (e.g., Chaplin, 2014; Lloyd, 2020; Shapira, 2015, 2020a; Wright, 2009).

The present Element is concerned with what I see as the completing countermove of the reclamation of trade Gothic: a growing curiosity about the lives of its authors. As I will describe (see Section 1.5), the recent interest in trade Gothic has manifested itself in a range of new discoveries about writers of Kelly's publishing profile, many (if not most) of whom were women. Nevertheless, we still know far less about trade-Gothic authors than we do about canonical ones such as Walpole, Lewis, Radcliffe or Shelley, all of whom have been the subjects of book-length scholarly biographies – multiple ones, in Lewis and Shelley's case (D.L. Macdonald, 2000; Mellor, 2012; Mowl, 2014; Norton, 1999; Peck, 1961; Seymour, 2011; Townshend, 2024).

But why does it matter? Why invest time and resources in expanding and deepening the biographies of trade-Gothic novelists? And – given the suspicion with which it has long been held – is authorial biography even a worthwhile pursuit? What, if anything, does it add to our understanding of Gothic writing and, more broadly, of Gothic literary history? These questions will be my concern in the introductory section, before moving on to Kelly as my extended case study.

1.1 Biography and Canonical Gothic

Biography has long had a questionable reputation among literary scholars. When the discipline of modern literary studies was first institutionalized in the early twentieth century, interest in authors' lives seemed a throwback to what Andrew Bennett calls 'the leisurely, dilettante pursuit of literature', a naive – if not vulgar – indulgence in 'gossip' (2005: 73). Biography was then dismissed by the mid century New Critics as part of the 'gross body of life, of sensory and mental experience' which, because external to the text, had no place in its analysis (Wimsatt and Beardsley, 1946: 479). It was later again pronounced irrelevant by poststructuralist thinkers, most prominently Roland Barthes, who protested, in 'The Death of the Author', against the 'image of literature ... tyrannically centred on the author, his person, his life, his tastes, his passions' (1977: 143). As the author has stubbornly lived on, however, biography has lingered as well. While the 'linkage between works and lives is complicated, multivalent, and at times limiting and destructive', Matthew Sangster writes, '... it still fundamentally underpins the ways in which twenty-first century readers assimilate what we read into our wider cultural understandings' (2021: 9). Biography thus remains what Richard Bradford calls 'the elephant in the room': 'it exists, is indeed sometimes practiced by peers and colleagues, but it owes rather too much to the vulgar undisciplined practices and tastes of the book world outside the academy' (Bradford, 2019: 340).

As a first step towards evaluating the necessity of biography in the case of trade-Gothic authors, it would help to recognize how central authorial lives, and the author figure more broadly, have been to the study of canonical Gothic. Demonstrating Michel Foucault's (1977) idea of an 'author function', authorship has provided a major way of organizing the Gothic's intricate history. Gothic authors have served the classificatory purposes that Foucault sees as essential to the author function: their names have represented important milestones in the Gothic's emergence and development, marked forks in the literary-historical road and served as labels under which Gothic texts might be grouped together or, conversely, differentiated from each other. The common debates over whether or not Horace Walpole truly was the 'first' Gothic author and the widespread critical practice of dividing 1790s Gothic into 'Radcliffean' and 'Lewisite' strands demonstrate the enduring usefulness of authors in describing, organizing and understanding the Gothic's evolution.

Moreover, the study of Gothic texts and Gothic literary history has been informed by a great deal of biographical information. Within Gothic literary criticism as it is commonly practised, *The Castle of Otranto* is located firmly within Horace Walpole's life as an upper-class man of letters, an aficionado of Gothic architecture, the builder of Strawberry Hill (e.g., Watt, 1999: 18–41). Walpole's suspected homosexuality, like that of Matthew Lewis and William Beckford, has played a role in readings of the three men's Gothic novels since the 1980s (e.g., Haggerty, 1986), just as Radcliffe's gender, class affiliation and dissenting background have factored into interpretations of her fiction (e.g., Miles, 1995; 2012). Mary Shelley's parentage, pregnancies, motherhood and marriage have for decades been common fodder for readers of *Frankenstein* (Duncker, 2004). This is not to say that Gothic studies as a discipline has necessarily practised biographical criticism in the overly simplistic sense of, in Sangster's words, 'seek[ing] definitive explanations of works in the lives of their authors' (8). But corollaries between authorial lives and the central themes of Gothic fiction have stubbornly presented themselves, and critics have responded to them with varying degrees of theorization and self-awareness. What does it mean that Walpole wrote *The Castle of Otranto* – the story of a man frantically trying to avoid the exposure of dark family secrets – soon after a controversy that cast doubt on his own masculinity and sexual orientation (Campbell, 1998)? Or could *Otranto* actually be reflecting Walpole's anxieties about his paternity (Williams, 2009)? Is Frankenstein a 'birth myth' that became 'lodged in the novelist's imagination … by the fact that she was herself a mother' (Moers, 1978: 92)? Does Charlotte Dacre's black demon-hero in *Zofloya, or, The Moor* (1806) have anything to do with her own identity as the daughter of a notorious Jew (Hoeveler, 1995)? These questions, and others like them, have been raised by scholars over the years, showing that authorial biography, although rarely flagged as a methodological choice, plays an ongoing and significant role in Gothic criticism.

1.2 Canonical Authorship and the Author–Text Cycle

The broader claim I wish to make here, drawing on the work of narratologist Susan S. Lanser (2003), is that biographical knowledge forms part of an idea of the author that informs our reading. According to Lanser, readers bring with them to any literary work a mental construct of the author created out of both textual and extra-textual information. The latter includes paratexts (e.g., authorial ascription, dedication, preface) and 'at least two distinct but related types of prior inferential knowledge', these being 'the assumptions about reliability, credibility and wisdom that a given culture confers on authorship, and some rudimentary sense of a particular authorial biography, even if "biography" is as limited as a suggestion of the author's sex or nationality' (Lanser, 2003: 84).

This mental construct is brought to bear on the text and further informed by it in turn, a dynamic that Lanser calls the 'tautological constructio[n] of authors and texts' (2003: 82), and that I will refer to as the 'author–text cycle'. Within this cycle, any new information about an author, or even just a different view of the author created by our own evolving perspective, will likely feed into the reading of the writing; conversely, a new and different understanding of the work or works (or – in a more exciting scenario – the discovery of a writer's previously unknown work) will in turn revise the figure of the author we hold in our heads. A conspicuous and instructive case of this cycle can be found in the case of Jane Austen, whose shifting critical fortunes have informed, and been informed by, an array of different authorial incarnations over the centuries – 'dear Aunt Jane', spinster Austen, conservative Austen, progressive Austen, feminist Austen, queer Austen (Johnson, 1996), and the list will likely still grow further. Each of these personae has nourished, and been nourished by, new readings of Austen's fiction.

To see how this cycle has worked in the case of Gothic authorship, we might turn to a key moment in the modern critical history of Austen's contemporary Ann Radcliffe. Today Radcliffe is an unequivocally canonical figure, widely discussed in scholarship and taught regularly at universities. Three decades ago, however, when Robert Miles published his groundbreaking study *Ann Radcliffe: The Great Enchantress* (1995), her scholarly reputation was still being consolidated. In his introduction, Miles pointed to what he saw as a stubborn gap between Radcliffe's achievements and her modern-day reception: even though Radcliffe was a 'huge, Europe-wide success' and 'one of the most influential novelists of her generation', critics remained 'ambivalent' about her writing (2). Miles' book sought to narrow this gap by showing that Radcliffe's novels have 'aesthetic depth' (3), 'engage critically with her society and culture' and 'possess a teasing, satisfying complexity' (4) – in short, that they meet the requirements for serious academic interest and appreciation. Before Miles could make his case, however, there was an obstacle he had to overcome. That obstacle, as he explained, was 'Mrs. Radcliffe'.

'Mrs. Radcliffe' is what Miles called Ann Radcliffe's 'fusty cognomen', the authorial persona into which she was 'subsumed' as soon as her novels stopped appearing anonymously (27). It stands for an image of Radcliffe which has circulated since the Romantic period – that of a proper middle-class wife, shy and retiring, scrupulous to a fault; a woman said to have valued decorum above all else, to have been a 'gentlewoman' first and an 'authoress' second. But this image, Miles argued, is not a definitive or verifiable biographical portrait of Radcliffe, about whom very little is known with certainty. 'Mrs. Radcliffe', rather, is the heroine of the particular version of Radcliffe's life told in the memoir that Thomas Noon Talfourd (1826) wrote after her death, apparently helped by her husband William, 'the jealous guardian of Mrs. Radcliffe's reputation' (Miles, 1995: 27.)

What concerned Miles about the enduring idea of 'Mrs. Radcliffe' was less its accuracy than its consequences for criticism. Attached to this familiar figure of Radcliffe, Miles argued, was a set of 'narrowly intentionalist prejudices' – a series of assumptions about what Radcliffe could and could not have been writing about, derived from the idea of who she supposedly was (20). 'If one were to take her first biographers at face value', Miles wrote,

> one would assume that 'Mrs Radcliffe' did successfully sink the 'authoress' in the 'gentlewoman,' that her social vision was conservative, that criticism of her betters was the last thing in the gentlewoman's mind, and that it would be quite improper to read into her depiction of European social disharmony refracted images of tensions close to home. (29)

A particular idea of the author, Miles suggested, can have a limiting effect on the interpretive horizon; critics reading Radcliffe's fiction with 'Mrs. Radcliffe' in mind would find only what they assumed that a 'Mrs. Radcliffe' could write.

But if Talfourd and William Radcliffe had woven one kind of story around the few known facts of Radcliffe's life, Miles showed, it was also possible to imagine another. This alternative story took into account Radcliffe's age (she was in her late twenties and early thirties when her major novels came out), her dissenting background and the radical intellectuals she likely met at the house of her uncle Thomas Bentley. The heroine of this story was not the decorous, conservative 'Mrs. Radcliffe' but a 'vibrant young novelist' who 'did not give in to the proper lady – at least, not without a struggle', and who 'may very well have sharpened her critical wits in the "dissident" milieu of the Bentley household' (27, 29). If the words in the fiction came from the pen of *that* Ann Radcliffe, it was far more understandable and believable that – as Miles' book argued – they could 'conceal a hard edge, one sharpened by the robust, liberal, critical energies of the dissenting "middling classes" to which she belonged' (4).

Miles' confrontation with 'Mrs Radcliffe' demonstrates how the author–text cycle works and why it matters. For Miles, the 'Mrs. Radcliffe' that many readers knew in 1995 stood in the way of fully appreciating Radcliffe's fiction; assumptions about the author, he believed, kept critics from accepting or even seeing certain interpretive possibilities. He was thus compelled to begin his book with a critique of Radcliffe's inherited portrait in order to loosen its hold on the perception of her novels. At the same time, Miles' very reason for challenging the figure of 'Mrs. Radcliffe' came from the clash between this figure and his own understanding of the work. If he had not seen Radcliffe's fiction as possessing qualities that seemed inconsistent with the common view of the author – such as, for example, a discerning and even critical view of contemporary political debates – he might not have felt the need to argue for a different Ann Radcliffe.

1.3 Canonization and the Ongoing Project of Biography

As the case of 'Mrs Radcliffe' demonstrates, the author–text cycle can play a crucial role in processes of canonization: the changing critical fortunes of authors are tied up in the changing critical views of their writing, and vice versa.

In the case of Gothic studies, biographical interest was part of the broader move to legitimize a canon by showing certain Gothic novels to be distinctive artworks, each tied to the particular vision of a specific author. Hard as it may seem to believe today, even those novels we now consider to be discrete peaks of Romantic-Gothic achievement – for example, Walpole's *The Castle of Otranto* (1764), Radcliffe's *The Mysteries of Udolpho* (1794) and Lewis' *The Monk* – were once regarded as essentially similar manifestations of the same regrettable popular fad. Challenging this view was one of the goals of early Gothic scholarship: David Punter opens his pioneering 1980 study *The Literature of Terror* by explaining that 'there are important differences between the better-known Gothic novels', which literary history 'has tended to group ... together into a homogeneous body of fiction' (Punter, 1996, 1: 1). Punter's monograph was a groundbreaking attempt to 'ungroup' these works, a critical endeavour that has since continued successfully for decades. Analysed, psychoanalysed, historicized, theorized, read and reread in contexts too numerous to survey, the canonical Gothic novels have by now become cultural monuments, each clearly itself even as it participates in broader historical trends. This individuation of texts has been buttressed by the ongoing interest in their creators, with authors' lives used to illuminate the idiosyncrasies of their work and illuminated by them in turn.

Critical interest and biographical research tend to boost one another: scholarly interest in an author's life tends to surge when the author's writing gains recognition and appreciation. At the same time, biographical projects – especially those that make historical sources (e.g., letters or diaries) more widely accessible – can ground and encourage new scholarship. As Christina Morin argued in her 2011 book on Maturin, the absence of a biographical context diminished critics' ability to appreciate Maturin's achievements: when reading is restricted by the 'general cultural ignorance ... [about] Maturin and the details of his life', Morin wrote, 'Maturin's works lose much of their immediacy, dependent as they frequently are on Maturin's personal religious and theological beliefs as well as his perspective on current affairs in Ireland, Britain and Europe'. In offering her own account of 'the major people, dates and places of Maturin's life', Morin thus aimed to 'provide a solid biographical basis for the discussion that follows', since – as she suggested – such a basis is required for his work to be fully appreciated by a modern reader (2011: 22).

Conversely, insufficient belief in an author's literary merit can have a stifling effect on biographical inquiry, as Peck himself discovered when he first tried to publish his Lewis biography. A letter preserved among Peck's papers at Harvard's Houghton Library reveals that his manuscript was rejected in 1959 by the Clarendon Press on the grounds that 'Monk Lewis is a relatively minor figure, unsuited to the kind of extended treatment you have given him' (Blake, 1959). Clearly the reader for Clarendon did not agree with Peck's claim that Lewis was coming to be recognized as 'an important figure not only among the Gothic writers of the period but in the realm of comparative literature as well' (Peck, 1961: v). Luckily, other readers and editors felt differently, and Peck's biography was published by Harvard University Press in 1961.

Academic interest in an author's work also contributes to the further enrichment and complication of the available biography. In the words of William St. Clair, 'the writing of biography is as much subject to what the Romantics called "the spirit of the age" as other forms of writing', so that 'updatings and reappraisals are ... a necessary part of each generation's attempt to reach its own understanding of the past' (St. Clair, 2004: 221). Lewis' case is, again, instructive. Precisely because – as Peck predicted – Lewis became an established part of academic study, *A Life of Matthew G. Lewis* eventually became unsatisfying, especially due to Peck's reluctance to discuss Lewis' sexuality. For a later generation of critics, who saw Romantic-era Gothic (and *The Monk* in particular) as a significant moment in queer literary history, sexual biography was an important issue, and could no longer simply be sidestepped. When D.L. Macdonald published his own Lewis biography in 2000, he therefore offered a new perspective on the question of Lewis' sexuality that was far better suited to the interests and needs of his contemporaries (Macdonald, 2000: 59–92; see also Townshend, 2024: 56–74).

Authorial biography, then, is not a stable, unchanging entity but a story which shifts and evolves over time – whether in order to provide answers to newly pressing questions or simply because successive biographers are driven to find what previous scholars had missed. Christina Rossetti longed to base her intended biography of Radcliffe on 'any hoard of diaries or correspondence hitherto unpublished' (Rossetti, 1883) – a wish that ended in disappointment, prompting Rossetti to give up the project. In his own biography of Radcliffe, Rictor Norton (1999) reiterated the challenge presented by the fact that 'Ann Radcliffe kept no diaries, other than some travel journals which contain very few personal details' (1); but, refusing to join the ranks of those who had been 'frightened off by Rossetti's estimation' (vii), he nonetheless tried to tell the story more fully, though his task, he admitted, was 'that of the detective, piecing together the clues' (2). Even when little new information is available, the author's figure often continues to develop, and what few biographical sources exist are plumbed repeatedly for new insight. And so Cheryl Nixon (2015), for example, uses Radcliffe's commonplace book to suggest an analogy between the account Radcliffe kept of her final illness and the Gothic heroine's experience of her body. In doing so, Nixon offers a new lens through which to read

Radcliffe's work; at the same time, she also adds to the evolving image of Radcliffe herself. The fact that this image keeps, indeed, evolving is evidence of the pull continually exerted by biographical material, with its always-tantalizing promise of access to the 'real' author lost to us in history.

The nearly half-century now of vigorous critical inquiry into the Gothic canon has thus been complemented by an equally vigorous desire to know and understand the creators of this canon. Biographical research about them has been done, and redone; new information has been discovered, and old information has been read anew. The author–text cycle has thus turned and turned for canonical authors and their novels, with ever more complex and individualized authorial figures emerging in dialogue with an evolving, deepening and widening view of their writing over time.

1.4 Trade Gothic and Authorship

In the case of trade Gothic, attempts to individuate both texts and authors have been slow to emerge. Like the overall critical antipathy towards trade-Gothic novels, the widespread perception of these works as forming a homogeneous mass is rooted in the Romantic period, when reviewers commonly described popular novels using such epithets as '"hordes," "swarms" and "shoals" – always plural and undifferentiated' (Ferris, 1991: 43; see also Peiser, 2020: 130–131). But modern scholars, too, have treated popular novels of the period as virtually interchangeable, and thus – in Elizabeth Neiman's pithy phrase – as somehow both '"already read" and not worth reading' (2019: 45). The persistence of this view is evident in the critical practice of using one novel to represent the entire trade-Gothic phenomenon; hence Punter's assertion that Lathom's *The Midnight Bell* (1798) is 'a single example... as good a one as any' that will 'hopefully... suffice to summarise many lesser works' (Punter, 1996, 1:114). The cursory attention paid to trade-Gothic novels has resulted in what Hannah Hudson describes as 'an increasing polarization: the "known" Gothic texts have become increasingly familiar and canonical, and the "unknown" ones have grown increasingly concrete as well – but as a body, not as individual works' (2013: 35).

The stubborn view of Romantic-era popular novels as interchangeable correlates to the similar treatment of these novels' authors as being somehow all the same – or at least, similar enough to each other that any one of them can represent the rest. This perception, too, has a very long history: just as they dismissively homogenized popular novels, Romantic-era critics depicted trade-Gothic authors using unflattering generalizations – for example, a 'vulgar herd' or, elsewhere 'those ladies who assiduously feed the pig-stye of literature in

Leadenhall-street', an allusion to the location of the Minerva offices in London (cited in Peiser, 2020: 130). Suffused with both gender- and class-based contempt, such language merged popular novelists into a faceless aggregate of menial labourers, the defining 'other' of the Romantic author – in Bennett's words, an ideal figure who is 'autonomous, original and expressive', set sharply apart from 'the idea of the writer, the scribbler, the journalist or literary drudge' (2005: 56, 60).

The homogenization of popular novelists extended into twentieth-century critical discourse. Describing William Lane as 'the largest employer of hack novelists – particularly women novelists – in the country', Nigel Cross in *The Common Writer: Life in Nineteenth Century Grub Street* (1988) presented Eliza Parsons as, in his words, 'as good an example as any' of the period's popular authors (168, 169). Parsons' fiction was of little interest to Cross; she served mainly as the embodiment of a certain type of author – what he called 'the female drudge' (Cross, 1988: 164), the woman author of badly written popular fare who is motivated only by financial desperation. While recent scholarship on the Romantic market for popular fiction has been far less dismissive, its tendency to offer big-picture views of the system within which popular novelists worked still tends to reduce individual writers to what Anthony Mandal calls 'cogs in great novel-producing machines like the Minerva Press' (2015: 27).

Mandal's metaphor points us back to a Romantic-era image that has been essential to the enduring perception of trade-Gothic authors as lacking significant individuality. 'Over and over again', Ina Ferris writes, 'the ordinary novel [of the Romantic period] is depicted as stamped out by machines, produced not by authors but by printing presses' (1991: 43). This notion of dehumanized mechanical production is captured in the common Romantic cliché of the printing press churning out novels on its own – the same cliché to which Austen's narrator refers in *Northanger Abbey* when she mocks the critics who 'talk in threadbare strains of the trash with which the press now groans' (2003: 23). Within this metaphor lie the seeds of a longtime critical practice, in which trade-Gothic writers are not really treated as 'authors' in the usual sense, that is, as human creators whose individuality matters for understanding their creation. As Ferris notes, the likening of authors to machines suggests that popular fiction is 'a discourse outside the author-function' (43); this conception of popular authorship (or perhaps non-authorship?) further discourages the study of popular authors as historical individuals. One machine, after all, is very much like another; to inquire into its life story would surely be beside the point.

Where trade Gothic is concerned, therefore, the traditional workings of the author–text cycle contributed not to canonization but to its opposite. We might recall here Lanser's claim, cited above, that 'the assumptions about reliability, credibility, and wisdom that a given culture confers on authorship' (Lanser, 2003: 84) inform the construction of the author that readers bring to bear on the text; in this case, it is the assumption that trade authors *lack* wisdom, along with talent and agency, that has long coloured the perception of their work. The author–text cycle has thus perpetuated the marginalization of trade novels through the mutually reinforcing ideas of, on the one hand, a literary corpus made up of near-identical commodities and, on the other hand, a cadre of barely known, seemingly interchangeable authors functioning in a quasi-mechanical fashion. Punter demonstrated the practical implications of this dynamic in 1980 when he contrasted the 'Gothic masters' with what he called 'Popular writers in the genre, [who] appear to have become increasingly able to turn out a formulaic product in a matter of weeks' (Punter, 1996, 1: 114). Having devoted to Radcliffe and Lewis a detailed chapter complete with biographical sketches for both, he then dismissed trade Gothic in two quick paragraphs, saying little about Lathom – his single 'representative' example – beyond the fact that he wrote both novels and plays.

1.5 Trade Gothic and Authorial Lives

As I argued (see Section 1.3), canonization and biographical research tend to boost and reinforce each other; so do marginalization and biographical obscurity. And indeed, biographies of trade authors have been slow to emerge. The Victorian compilers of the first edition of the *Dictionary of National Biography* (Stephen and Lee, 1885–1900) did take note of some of them, including short entries on Bennett, Bonhôte, Lathom, Meeke, Roche and Parsons.[2] These accounts, however, were based on extremely partial, sometimes unreliable information, as pithily demonstrated by the *DNB*'s description of Anna Maria Bennett, misnamed 'Agnes', as 'a married lady with many children, who survived her; but there is no evidence of her birth, her parentage, or her condition' (Stephen and Lee, 1885–1900, 4: 240). Elizabeth Meeke, the most prolific novelist of the Romantic period, appeared in the *DNB* as 'Mary Meeke', thought to be the wife of a clergyman – an error corrected only recently, when Simon Macdonald (2013) identified her as Frances Burney's stepsister, the former Elizabeth Allen.

The situation has improved in the last two decades, thanks to the new *Oxford Dictionary of National Biography* (Cannadine, 2004) and the growing amount of biographical research available through other reference works. In the case of

---

[2] The entries are found in the first edition of the *Dictionary of National Biography* (Stephen and Lee, 1885–1900), as follows: 'BENNETT, AGNES [*sic*] MARIA' (4: 240-241); 'BONHOTE, ELIZABETH' (5: 345–346); 'LATHOM, FRANCIS' (32: 170–171); 'MEEKE, Mrs. MARY' (37: 210); 'ROCHE, Mrs. REGINA MARIA' (49: 71); 'PARSONS, Mrs. Eliza' (43: 399).

women writers, the *Orlando: Women's Writing in the British Isles from the Beginnings to the Present* database (Brown, Clements and Grundy, 2024a) has been particularly significant as a biographical resource. Studies of individual trade authors and particular trade novels have also added to what we know about their lives, updating the colourful (if not always accurate) biographical sketches compiled in the twentieth century by Montague Summers (1963) and Devendra P. Varma (1966).[3]

Along with this new biographical surge, there has been a gradual recognition of the light that biographical knowledge can shed on trade Gothic. Punter, who articulated the stark terms of the canon/trade divide and its implications for authorial biography in 1980, deserves credit for his early contribution to the rethinking of this divide. In a 2003 article, Punter and Alan Bissett explored the critical insights that arise when *The Midnight Bell* is read vis-à-vis Lathom's 'impossible biography' (55). Lathom was a successful Norwich playwright who abruptly left his theatre career and moved to the Scottish countryside, possibly due to the exposure of a homosexual relationship. How, Lathom and Bisset asked, might this personal backstory – itself 'a construct, a narrative' (56) – illuminate Lathom's formulaic novel? Might the 'curious entanglement of secrecy and display' (57) in Lathom's life story shed light on the Gothic elements of his novel – repressed family secrets, forbidden desire, imprisonment and the yearning to escape?

What Punter and Bissett demonstrated is what other scholars have both learned and showed: that formulaic fiction often becomes more interesting and meaningful when read vis-à-vis an author whom the scholar has made some effort to individuate. And so the discovery that Horsley Curties was a Yeoman of the Guard leads Townshend (2008) to the recognition that he was engaged in 'two entirely incompatible if not mutually exclusive activities: a professional commitment to the Hanoverian Monarchy... and a semi-professional dabbling in the subversive ways of Gothic romance' (7). Biographical discovery thus helps Townshend to explain the idiosyncratic nature of Horsley Curties' fiction, which 'seems more intent upon conserving the patriarchal institutions of fatherhood and sovereign power than subverting them in the tradition of countless, more radical Gothic romances of the 1790s' (7). Morin similarly illuminates Roche's Gothic fiction by placing it in the immediate biographical context of her 'experiences as an émigré author in London' (2018: 155) and thus also in the broader context of Irish participation in the global literary trade.

---

[3] Karen Morton's 2011 book on Parsons remains the only book-length study of a trade author of which I am aware. In addition to work on trade-Gothic authors cited below, see also Czlapinski and Wheeler (2011); DeLucia (2020); Mackley (2021); Mandal (2018); and Potter (2005: 110–116, 132–134).

Gender, nationality, class, geographical location, personal history, education, religion, professional and literary experience – all these and other biographical factors can thus contribute to a thickened authorial portrait, which can replace the generic sketch of the trade-Gothic author as faceless 'drudge'. When read with such a portrait in mind, seemingly generic features of the text likewise take on additional possible meanings, and the fiction, too, begins to seem less bland. But the process is, of course, cyclical: recognizing the idiosyncrasies of a text or oeuvre in turn helps to bring the author into relief as an individual making a particular set of choices. The more we know about that individual, the more legible and, indeed, even *visible* those choices become.

To answer my own question in opening, biography matters for trade-Gothic authors because its absence matters: our lack of knowledge about trade authors as historical individuals affects the way we read their novels, and it also affects our broader view of Gothic literary history in the Romantic period. Holding on to the view of trade writers as a cadre of faceless, interchangeable drudges has entrenched the mass dismissal of their novels as equally indistinct, interchangeable 'imitations'. It has also shaped our understanding of their relation to canonical authors: in their well-developed biographical roundness, the latter have naturally seemed like the central protagonists of the literary-historical narrative, while the minimally sketched trade authors have just as naturally been the supporting characters of whom no one expects very much. Biographical research into trade authors interrupts this long-time dynamic, revealing an individuality among them that makes it easier to see idiosyncrasy, nuance and particular emphases in their novels. And it also, as I will show (see Section 4), sometimes allows us to tell different stories about the Gothic – stories in which trade authors play a larger role in terms of contribution and influence than we have previously believed possible.

In the three sections that follow, I will use Kelly's case to demonstrate how a more complex biographical portrait of an author can change the way we read trade-Gothic novels, while also adding nuance to our broader view of Romantic-Gothic literary history. But first, it is important to establish how challenging it is to create richer portraits of trade novelists, given the kind of sources in which information about their lives can be found. To go beyond the limitations imposed by these sources requires that we read biography and fiction side by side, tracing their mutual implications and indulging in the occasional bit of acknowledged speculation.

2 Isabella Kelly's Cover Stories

Isabella Kelly, née Fordyce, was descended from a prestigious Scottish lineage. In 1789 she married Captain Robert Hawke Kelly (d. 1807?), the son of Colonel

Robert Kelly (1738–1790) of the East India Company, expecting a life of genteel comfort, but soon found herself in ongoing financial difficulty. After Colonel Kelly's death the couple sunk into debt, and Robert was eventually imprisoned. With three children to raise and a husband who had what she would later describe as 'expensive habits' (Kelly, 1832), she struggled for years to make ends meet, a fact reflected no doubt in the pace of her fiction-publishing career: ten of her eleven novels appeared almost annually from 1794 to 1805. Eventually Robert took an appointment in the West Indies and died there. A short second marriage left Isabella widowed and in debt again, and she was still trying to make money by writing in her seventies, by which point she was supporting a grown daughter and grandchildren as well. She died in 1857, at the age of nearly 100.

The existing biographical accounts of Kelly thus all tell the story of a woman who spent decades in financial and personal distress, and whose prolific career as a novelist was undoubtedly fuelled by economic need (see Behrendt, 2002; Todd, 1985: 183–184; Nicholls and LeMay, 1993: 371; Brown, Clements and Grundy, 2024b; Lonsdale, 1989: 481–482; 'Kelly, Isabella', 2015; Greene, 2004; Raisanen, 2024). Reading this chronicle of woes, it is easy to understand Elizabeth Raisanen's claim that Kelly's life, 'filled with tragedy, poverty, and disappointment, mirrored the storylines of her persecuted female characters' (1); Stephen Behrendt likewise observes that Kelly's biography 'seems in many respects almost to have been drawn from the plots of her own novels'. Kelly's various misfortunes *do* resemble the serial ordeals of a heroine of sensibility, and they also resemble the biographies of other popular woman writers. Parsons, too, became a novelist in the wake of personal tragedies and struggled for decades with poverty and bad health (Morton, 2011: 45–59). Even the extremely popular Roche eventually found herself in financial trouble, describing to the Royal Literary Fund how her husband's illness and death had left her 'at once the most destitute and afflicted of human beings' (Roche, 1830). The details of these novelists' lives do seem oddly interchangeable, offering instance after instance of women defined exclusively by their serial distresses.

Kelly's existing authorial portrait, like those of other authors of her publishing profile, brings to mind E. M. Forster's famous distinction between 'flat' and 'round' characters (Forster, 1927: 65–75). Although Forster and the theorists who later debated and refined his terms focused on fiction, the distinctions they drew between different kinds of literary characters are useful for thinking about authorial biography. Like literary characters, authorial portraits are not all made equal; and about these, too, we might ask how wide a range of traits they include, whether they are 'presented from varied points of view', whether they are introduced to us using 'a "showing" or a "telling" technique' or whether they give us access to the interior of consciousness (Fishelov, 1990: 425). A criterion of particular importance for my purposes involves the degree of individuation: we may, as David Fishelov writes, 'perceive some character as typical', a 'representative of some social or psychological or even physical "property"' whose 'value and function can be summarized and exhausted in one brief phrase (for example, the jealous husband, the dumb blonde, or the spinster, etc.)' (422). The further a character moves from typicality into individuality, the 'rounder' it becomes, growing less predictable, more complex and contradictory, and possessing more of – as Forster puts it – 'the incalculability of life' (75).

The life stories we have of many trade-Gothic novelists indeed make them seem like the interchangeable iterations of a type. Yet because Kelly, Parsons and Roche are not literary inventions, since they undoubtedly did once possess the full 'incalculability of life', their 'flatness' is necessarily a matter of representation. Its cause becomes easy to understand once we take into account the sources in which biographical information about them has been preserved, sources that – as this section will show – have an inherently 'flattening' effect on what were once full, complex human beings.

Though for some long-neglected authors there is an abundance of biographical material – such as the archive of Jane Porter and Anna Maria Porter, subjects of a recent biography by Devoney Looser (2022) – Kelly's case is probably more typical. What we know about her comes from a limited number of documents, foremost among them her two applications to the Royal Literary Fund (Kelly, 1828a, 1828b; 1832). She also appears briefly in the letters and biographies of her patron Matthew Lewis (Baron Wilson, 1839, 1: 270–281; Peck 1961: 62–66; D.L. Macdonald, 2000: 60–63; Townshend, 2024: 30–33), and some additional biographical details can be found in the prefaces and dedications of her published books.

My own research has uncovered a few additional sources, including a letter that Kelly sent to Warren Hastings, the first British governor-general of India and a friend of her late father-in-law (Kelly, 1795a), as well as Colonel Kelly's will and letters that he and his son Robert wrote to the East India Company (R. Kelly, 1781, 1790; R.H. Kelly, 1793). But even with these new findings, virtually all the information we have about Kelly still comes from the archives of individuals and organizations to whom she was little more than a needy dependent. There is no other material for a biographer to work with: no journals, no intimate letters to friends or family, no annotated copies of Kelly's books.

The fact that what we know about Kelly comes mainly from the archives of benefactors has a crucial effect on the way she is remembered. The documents found in such archives were shaped by the purposes for which they were written, and as such they are inherently limiting, even distorting. As Jennie

Batchelor has shown, women applying to the Royal Literary Fund needed to be cautious in negotiating with an increasingly masculinized rhetoric of authorial 'genius', which they did in part by couching their assertions of professionalism 'in the reassuringly benign rhetoric of female sensibility' (2005: 507). We can see the same dynamic at work in Kelly's appeals to other benefactors: whatever her ambitions might have been, it was surely prudent for her to present herself to Lewis as 'poor Mrs. K[elly]', telling him – as he describes in a letter to his mother – that 'if she could but procure for her children the common necessaries of life by hard labour, she would prefer it to the odious task of writing' (Baron Wilson, 1: 277–278). The glimpses we have of Kelly thus all show a woman contorted into the limited poses allowed to her by the conjoined restrictions of gender, class and financial dependency. Of course what we hear is a litany of woes; of course, Kelly stresses her poverty, her suffering, her children's needs, her bad health. Those were the aspects of her life she needed to emphasize in the 'cover stories' she told to potential patrons, while leaving out any detail, sentiment or emotion that might have made her less sympathetic.

Is Kelly, then, doomed to flatness? And does this mean that her fiction – like that of her fellow popular novelists – can never have a complex author figure to complicate it, and be complicated by it in turn? No, I would argue; but given the dearth of sources, creating a 'rounder' picture of Kelly will require us to look critically at the images of her preserved in the archive, cross-referencing them with each other and with her published writing. As I will show, this method allows us to detect the silences, elisions and (in places) outright inventions which enabled Kelly to remain an unthreatening 'female drudge' to her potential patrons.

2.1 'With drooping wings and languid eyes'

Kelly learned about the necessity and power of strategic self-portrayal at a young age. As she was proud to mention in her various applications for help, she was '[d]escended from the first families in Scotland', related through her mother to the Fraser and Argyll clans (Kelly, 1832). Lineage, however, did not mean wealth: the elopement of her parents, William Fordyce (b. 1734) and Elizabeth Fraser (d. 1785), cut them off from their families. Her father entered the military, rising to the rank of captain in the Royal Marines, and later became groom of the bedchamber to George III (see Greene). When he lost that position, the family's financial situation apparently became desperate.

This unfortunate turn of events is described, albeit in coded form, in 'The Eagle, the Kite, and the Cock. An Emblematic Fable', one of two long autobiographical poems that Kelly included in her 1794 collection. Having claimed in the preface that her father was 'injured and oppressed by the unfeeling hand of Power' (Kelly, 1794a: iii–iv), she uses 'The Eagle, the Kite, and the Cock' to unfold a more detailed story of William Fordyce's fall from favour at court, told (somewhat bathetically) as a fable about birds – the 'Cock', his 'partlet' and their 'numerous happy flock' of 'nineteen chicks' (61).

Having served the father of the ruling 'Eagle', 'fought their battles' and 'spilt his blood', the Cock gains a position in the Eagle's service thanks to a patron, 'a bird of noble race' (61). But when the noble patron retires from court, he is replaced by 'a dissembling, cruel Kite' (60), who exploits the Cock's absence following his wife's death and gives his position away. The devastated father then calls on his 'eldest chick' (65) and sends her on a mission to court. 'The plea of innocence can't fail', he tells her, imploring: 'Exert thyself, a parent's need / Will teach a daughter how to plead' (66). Ever dutiful, the 'chick' rushes to the Kite and tearfully begs him to restore her father to his position. When the Kite refuses and accuses her father of corruption, she responds with 'honest pride' and 'indignant eyes', asserting her father's innocence and reminding the Kite that he will be judged by God (68). The Kite is unmoved, and the family's situation remains dire: the father is left 'Expos'd to sorrow, want, and debt', while his children are 'Scatter'd, neglected, hopeless driven' and forced to 'gain the hard-earn'd daily bread / ... Their virtues hid, their friends estranged' (69).

What Kelly describes in the poem is, apparently, her own origin story – the story of how she learned to use her eloquence in the service of her family's needs. Although the *Dictionary of National Biography* (Nicholls and LeMay, 371; Greene, 2004) claims that Isabella Fordyce was the youngest of three sisters, this does not appear to be the case. She did have two sisters, Margaret and Amelia (Lonsdale, 1989: 481), but baptism records suggest that they were both younger than her (*Margaret Jemima Fordice,* 1760; *Amelia Elizabeth Mary Fordice*, 1768). While I have not been able to confirm that the Fordyces – like the Cock and Partlet – had nineteen children, I have found baptism records for five sons born to William and Elizabeth Fordyce (sometimes spelled 'Fordice' in parish records) from 1753 to 1767, suggesting that theirs was a large family indeed.[4] Isabella was not the eldest child, but she apparently was the eldest daughter – and thus, according to the poem, the one sent to court to plead her father's case. Familial distress thus gave rise to Kelly's

---

[4] The findmypast.co.uk database contains baptism records for Thomas Fordyce, son of William Fordyce and 'Eliz. Fraser', Aberdeen, 1753; William Robert, Westminster, 1761; Alexander Heathcote Fordyce, 1763, Chelsea; Wymes Fordyce, 1765, and Owen Charles, 1767, both listed as the children of 'Captain' William Fordice and 'Elizabeth Frazer' and baptized in Edinburgh. See bibliography for full references.

public voice, a careful balance of the dignified and the pitiful that she would continue to maintain in appeals for help throughout her life.

Kelly, however, is present in the poem in more than one way: while embodied in the tearful 'chick', she is also represented by the knowing, detached voice of the poem's speaker. Confidently narrating the episode in iambic tetrameter, the speaker recognizes that feminine misery can, in fact, be a source of power under circumstances of powerlessness. As she says of the chick, 'Her meekness pleas'd – her looks prevail, / For when did ever meekness fail?' (Kelly 1794a: 66). Did Kelly herself have this sense of doubleness as the events described unfolded? Did she perform the role of weeping supplicant, while at the same time watching herself perform that role, gauging its impact, storing away the lesson for future use? We will never know for sure, but the very possibility suggests a complexity that the sentimental self-portrait alone cannot convey.

The speaker also wields power in the poem, though of a different nature than that exerted by the pitiful chick: hers is the power of the calculating storyteller, who finds covert ways to expose the misdeeds of the powerful. For the first time – but not the last – in her career, Kelly uses an apparent fiction to hint at life events that she is precluded from describing explicitly. Scattering clues through the fiction, the poem's speaker invites readers to connect the various birds to real-life referents. The 'bird of noble race' whose patronage secures the Cock's position at court is represented in places by the dashed-out names 'C——y' and 'H——d' (62), and he is said to live in 'R–l–y's peaceful shade' (61). The 'Kite', who comes from '*Hatfield's* woods', succeeds the noble patron as 'L——d C——b——n' (60) – a reference, clearly, to the position of Lord Chamberlain, and thus a clue to the likely identity of the two men. 'C——y', 'H——d' and 'R–l–y' correlate to Francis Seymour Conway (1718–1794), 1st Marquess of Hertford, whose ancestral estate was Ragley Hall; he served as Lord Chamberlain from 1766 to 1782, and briefly again in 1783. James Cecil (1748–1823), the 7th Earl (later 1st Marquess) of Salisbury, was Lord Chamberlain from 1783 to 1804. Hatfield, which Kelly names openly in the poem, was one of the Cecil family seats, a detail which points to the Earl as the man who had William Fordyce removed from his position; yet Kelly also seems to hedge her bets, adding a footnote which reads, 'It is not to be supposed this alludes to the present most noble Marquis of S——y' (1794a: 60).

Kelly thus delivers her self-portrait as the weepy, loyal daughter in a voice that evokes an altogether different persona – that of the author of the 'secret history', an apparent fiction with recognizable real-life referents. Usually associated with such early eighteenth-century writers as Aphra Behn and Delarivier Manley, the secret history continued to flourish and evolve into the 1800s and beyond (see Burgess, 2017), and Kelly made use of its possibilities on more than one occasion. The narrator of a secret history is, by definition, a knowing one, possessing inside information about the workings of power; because this information is dangerous and subversive, it can only be disclosed in code. Kelly's speaker, indeed, suggests this kind of inside knowledge when she claims that when the Cock lost his place at court, 'birds there were (perhaps too bold) / Declar'd, Lord Kite the place had sold' (1794a: 65). Worldly and unsentimental about the goings-on at court, the speaker invites readers who are 'in the loop' to trace the lineaments of real-life scandal.

To the two versions of Kelly in the poem – the weepy chick, and the knowing speaker – we need to add a third, implicit one: that of Kelly herself, the historical author outside the text, whom the poem invites us to imagine at three different moments. The earliest is Kelly some time after 1783, when Conway left court, William lost his job, and Isabella, a young woman in her mid twenties, was sent to plead on his behalf. Then there is Kelly in 1788, the year to which the poem is dated; now in her late twenties, having somewhat processed the experience, she chooses to write about it in a 'fable' that offers a coded exposé of court scandal.

Finally we have Kelly in 1794, when the book is published. This older Kelly has been married for five years, has lost a child, is likely pregnant with another (William Kelly was born in January 1795); she has also – as I will shortly describe – experienced a bitter personal and financial disappointment in her marriage. Looking for new sources of income, she publishes a poetry book, gathering subscribers among the Scottish aristocracy and gentry, friends in the military and distinguished relatives. This is Kelly putting the lessons learned by the 'chick' into action: concluding her sad tale of the 'Cock' and his offspring, she addresses those 'in fortune's favour high' and implores them to 'Be kind — protect a parent's age, / In his defence, ye good, engage!' (70, 71). The poem thus not only contains biographical information; it *is*, in its very writing and publication, a clue as to who Kelly was, revealing the calculating, canny agent behind the requisite sentimental performance.

2.2 'My Robert'

Kelly's marriage to Captain Robert Hawke Kelly gave her numerous opportunities to practice her skill of crafting 'cover stories', turning the messiness of life into a sympathetic appeal for assistance. Writing to Hastings in 1795, she described Robert's history in the following terms:

> Mr Kelly was bred to arms, tho a very liberal education accomplished him for any condition he served several years in India and fought by his fathers [*sic*] side, and for some military atchievement [*sic*] was appointed captain of the body guard to Sir Archibald Campbell; that situation he lost by returning to

England, as well for the securing of his health as to present the coll's [*sic*] maps to the Company; at that period we married and were going to India when the fatal tidings of his fathers [*sic*] death reached us[.] (Kelly, 1795a: fol. 93 verso).

In her Royal Literary Fund application almost thirty years later, Kelly would repeat some of the same story, adding a few other details:

> early in life I was married to the eldest son of Col. Kelly who died in the command of the Centre army at the siege of Seringapatam: that gave the first blow to our independence: my husband then in the Cavalry could not support his rank as he had done (for a mystery... involves Col. Kelly's fortune). (Kelly, 1832)

A variety of sources support the story Kelly tells here; they also, however, show where she embellishes, evades or downright fabricates. Colonel Robert Kelly Sr. (1738–1790) had a distinguished career as an infantry officer in India, taking part in the geographical surveying project that was part of Britain's growing control over Indian territory (Phillimore, 1946-1958, 1: 342). Robert, his eldest son, was born in India, but his childhood and youth apparently passed in England under the protection of Edward Hawke, 1st Baron Hawke (1705–1781), a naval war hero who – according to Isabella Kelly – 'loved [Robert] as a son, and brought him up in this country' and 'had as a school Boy given him an annuity', which was later doubled by his son, the 2nd Baron Hawke (Kelly, 1832).

When Isabella first met Robert, his prospects seemed good: his father had done well in India, and Robert himself had benefitted for years from the privilege and influence exerted on his behalf. Shortly after the first Lord Hawke's death in 1781, Colonel Kelly wrote to Company officials in Madras, presenting his son as the possessor of 'a military genius' and recommending him for the position of junior cadet – a rank created as a perk for officers and surgeons in India, who could thus secure a place for their sons within the military establishment (R. Kelly, 1781: fol. 413; Sutton, 2013). Robert served in India from 1782 to 1789, at which point he claimed to have been 'seized with a dangerous illness' and forced to return to England (R.H. Kelly, 1793: fols. 8b-9a). What happened next changed the course of his life – and, more importantly for my purposes, of Isabella's life, placing her on the path that would lead to her literary career and beyond.

Robert and Isabella were married at St. James' Church in Clerkenwell on 14th November 1789 (*Robert Kelly and Isabella Fordice*, 1789). Less than a year later, in July 1790, Colonel Kelly changed his will. Going systematically through the document, the colonel crossed out Robert's name wherever it appeared and amended the division of his assets between his children so as to exclude his eldest son. In a furious letter to his executor, he explained that he had 'Mutilated' the will 'on Account of the infamous ill behaviour of that undutiful Boy', who had behaved in an 'ungrateful and undutiful' manner towards 'Lord Hawke, to whom he owed more than filial duty and affection' (R. Kelly, 1790: fol. 16). There is no mention of his son's new wife, whose hopes of ease and prosperity had thus vanished. Two months later, on 29 September 1790, Colonel Kelly was killed (Phillimore, 1946–1958, 1: 344).

Was the Kellys' marriage itself the offence that caused the colonel to disown Robert? A clue pointing in that direction can be found in another autobiographical 'fable' included among Kelly's poems, 'The Hawk, the Magpie, and the Pigeons', which describes a 'pigeon' brought 'From India's clime to Britain's shade' to be sheltered by a 'noble Hawk', who is succeeded after his death by an equally generous son – clearly, a reference to Robert and the two Lord Hawkes (Kelly, 1794a: 55). But then, the poem recounts, the pigeon "took a wife, / More dear than liberty or life'; the Hawk is initially dismayed by the marriage, in which he 'Perceived his views, his wishes cros't' (55), but he remains generous towards the pigeons, even though they behave with a 'vain extravagance' that they come to regret (56). Assuming that the poem describes Robert and Isabella's marriage, it is possible that Colonel Kelly was less forgiving of this 'extravagance' than Lord Hawke or perhaps infuriated by the marriage itself, especially if it contradicted their patron's wishes.

Whatever its causes, the loss of the Colonel's support, along with Robert's expected fortune, was a turning point in the couple's life, depriving Robert not only of his inheritance but of his connection within the East India Company. In a frantic attempt to recoup some of his losses Robert wrote to the Company in 1793, presenting himself as his father's assistant in his surveying efforts, with no mention of the rupture between them. He claimed that he had returned to England in 1789 not only to recuperate from his illness but to present Company officials with 'a set of maps of the Carnatick compiled by the Colonel his [i.e., the petitioner's] father with vast Expence, much labor and great study; in which work your petitioner assisted in the intervals of his military occupations' (R. H. Kelly, 1793: fol. 9a). That plan, Captain Kelly claimed, had been foiled by 'the sudden & Melancholy death of his father', after which the maps had been claimed by Colonel Kelly's executor. Carefully sidestepping his estrangement from his father, Robert begs the 'Hon[oura]ble Board' to 'grant him a provision in whatever manner their in their Goodness & Wisdom may deem meet' and mentions 'a Wife in a most destitute Condition' – the single, nameless reference to Isabella Kelly in the documents that set the course of her life (fol. 9b).

Within only a short time of her marriage, then, Kelly once again found herself needing to beg for help; this time, however, she faced the added challenge of hiding certain embarrassing facts. Both she and Robert saw fit to disguise the circumstances of the Colonel's death: Robert claimed that his father's life had been 'cut off by treachery (being poisoned) while in command of the center division' (R.H. Kelly, 1793: fol. 9a), while Isabella's letter to Snow stated that he 'died in the command of the Centre army at the siege of Seringapatam' (Kelly, 1832). By the time she wrote to Snow in 1832, Kelly had reason to hope that he would accept as fact the Colonel's alleged death at Seringapatam (Srirangapatna), which the British had besieged in 1792 and again in 1799. The Colonel, however, was already dead by September 1790, and under far less heroic circumstances: he was killed in a duel with a fellow officer, whom he reportedly challenged after the latter referred to him as an 'old woman' (Phillimore, 1946-1958, 1: 344). Apparently, such a manner of death was unhelpful when asking for sympathy and assistance; some artful tweaking was necessary.

But the bigger challenge, for Kelly, was how to present her husband's situation when trying to secure financial help and patronage. Robert's disinheritance was a disgrace that, as far as I know, she never publicly admitted: the closest she came was the allusion, in the preface to her poems, to '*a husband neglected by those on whom he had hereditary claims of protection*' (Kelly, 1794a: iv). Everywhere else she was far more evasive. Writing to Hastings in 1795, when the falling-out was still relatively fresh and possibly already known to Hastings, she simply avoided the matter, describing Robert only as 'the first born darling of your gallant, <u>ever</u> admiring friend' while making no mention of the rift between the 'first born darling' and his late father (Kelly, 1795a: fol. 93 verso, emphasis in original). In her letter to Snow nearly three decades later she was still vague, claiming that 'a mystery … involves Col. Kelly's fortune' (Kelly, 1832). As I will discuss in the next section, Kelly eventually wrote her most candid account of the marriage to Robert under the guise of fiction in her novel *Ruthinglenne, or, the Critical Moment* (1801); yet even there, she obfuscated. 'General Montgomery', Colonel Kelly's fictionalized counterpart, leaves his son 'Captain Montgomery' £20,000 in his will, before the money mysteriously disappears (Kelly, 1801, 2: 246). Even in fiction, this particular truth could not be told.

Robert's behaviour after the falling-out with his father also required Kelly to choose her words carefully. Matthew Lewis' first biographer, Margaret Baron Wilson, showed no such reticence when she described how Robert, having found himself in reduced circumstances, 'continued to pursue an idle and even dissipated course' (1: 271). In the years that followed Robert's disinheritance, the Kellys had three children: William Henry Martin Dillon (b. 1795); Fitzroy Edward (1796–1880), who grew up to become Sir Fitzroy Kelly, a respected judge and politician; and Amel Rosa (b. 1800; see Townshend, 2024: 59, 34).

We can only imagine how Kelly must have felt as her family grew and her husband proved consistently unreliable. Yet she was always circumspect when describing Robert's conduct, perhaps worried that openly criticizing him would make her seem less sympathetic.

For a genteel woman, sharing details of the marital breakdown that left her in need was a risky move: when Charlotte Smith wrote candidly to the Earl of Egremont about her husband's debaucheries, the Earl – according to Judith Stanton – 'found her reports... unacceptably haranguing and indiscreet' (17). Kelly may have feared a similar recoiling when she chose to minimize her references to Robert's indiscretions. In the letter to Hastings her tone is that of a loving wife lamenting the fact that 'my Robert', though 'qualified for any capacity', is unable to find employment (Kelly, 1795a: fol. 94 recto). Even decades later, when writing to Snow, she remains reticent, mentioning only the adverse affects of 'expensive habits', without attributing them to anyone in particular (Kelly, 1832).

Kelly's appeals to the Royal Literary Fund, moreover, take pains to blur the fact that Robert's inadequacies forced her to write for money even before his death. In her first application she mentions only that 'Early in life left an officers [*sic*] unprovided widow, the exertions of my pen enabled me to support and educate my children' (Kelly, 1828a). In the letter to Snow she describes how Robert accepted a position in the West Indies and died there soon after his arrival, leaving her 'a widow with three infants to support and educate' and 'no resource but my pen' (Kelly, 1832). Through this careful wording, Kelly avoids acknowledging what the letter to Hastings clearly establishes: that she began to write not because of Robert's death but because of his failures, stepping in to assume the financial responsibilities that he neglected.

Kelly's descriptions of her first husband disguise not only facts but feelings: her self-censorship leaves out the full experience of the ordeal, which surely aroused sentiments other than wifely devotion. With no surviving archive of private letters, we have no access to any freer expressions of the outrage and frustration she surely felt. In Kelly's fiction, however, we can occasionally find her anger voiced in coded form, thus restoring to her a basic emotion essential for human 'roundness'. As I will discuss in Section 3, Kelly hinted at marital struggle in her poems, and she eventually wrote a scathing account of her life with Robert, thinly fictionalized, in *Ruthinglenne*. A more oblique allusion to the outrageous cost that women pay for men's misbehaviour appears in Kelly's dedication of her novel *Joscelina, or, the Rewards of Benevolence* (1797) to the Duchess of York. Declaring herself 'grateful, proud, and happy' to be allowed to dedicate the book to the Duchess, she adds that 'while the trembling wife venerates the Royal munificence which may extricate a husband from distress, the anxious mother blesses the gracious hand which preserves her infants' (Kelly, 1798, I: iv).

It would seem apparent that the distressed husband mentioned here is Robert; yet given the identity of her dedicatee, Kelly's words raise another possibility. After the Duchess of York (born Princess Frederica of Prussia) had married Frederick, Duke of York, in 1791, the press made much of her role in covering her husband's gambling debts (Morris, 1996: 523). A 1792 satirical print by Isaac Cruikshank (see Figure 1) shows her sitting across a table from the Duke and handing him a box of jewels; a bill for £17,000 is visible on the table, while the written text above the Duchess' head declares, 'My Jewels? trifles! not worth the speaking of, if weigh'd against a husband's peace.' While thanking the Duchess for her patronage, Kelly in her *Joscelina* dedication implicitly links Robert to the reckless accumulation of debt for which the Duke (like his brother, the Prince of Wales) was notorious. She thus also reminds readers that any woman – even a princess – might find herself called upon to make up for her husband's profligacy, through no fault of her own.

Although we know little about Kelly's second marriage, evidence suggests that history repeated itself with painful accuracy. On 22 May 1809, she married Joseph

Figure 1 Isaac Cruikshank, *A Scene in the Gamester*, 1792. The Yale Center for British Art, Yale University. https://collections.library.yale.edu/catalog/10732736. Access and usage rights: Public.[5]

---

[5] The alt text in the electronic version of this Element is based on the description in the British Library catalogue, https://www.britishmuseum.org/collection/object/P_J-3-80.

Hedgeland at St. Luke's Church in Chelsea (*Joseph Hedgeland and Isabella Kelly*, 1809). We catch a brief glimpse of Kelly at this period in her life in the writing of journalist William Jerdan (1782–1869), who described living across from Joseph Hedgeland and his wife, 'better known as Isabella Kelly, the authoress of some popular novels' (1852–1853, 1: 102). Jerdan referred to Hedgeland as a 'tea grocer', though Fitzroy Kelly – whom he apparently knew – insisted later that his stepfather had advanced to the more prosperous status of 'merchant' (Jerdan, 1869: 783). Yet whatever wealth and respectability Hedgeland had accumulated, he apparently soon lost. A postscript to one of Kelly's letters to the Royal Literary Fund reads: 'One short year was the wife of Mr. Hedgeland, a fatal confidence and speculation lost his fortune and broke his heart' (Kelly, 1828b).

It is not clear why Kelly reduces to 'one short year' what was, in fact, a three-year marriage: records clearly show that the couple married in 1809, and that Joseph Hedgeland died three years later (*Joseph Hedgeland*, 1812). Kelly's strategies in writing about her first marriage, however, offer a possible clue. Kelly resumed her literary career before Joseph's death, publishing *Literary Information; consisting of instructive Anecdotes, Explanations, and Derivation*s in 1811.[6] She may have preferred to let the Fund's gentlemen ponder her tragically short second marriage rather than admit that, once again, she had gone to work to make up for a husband's financial failure. However disillusioned she might have been with marriage by this point, the cover story of the dutiful wife needed to stay intact – in her appeals for help, at least. Her fiction, as we will see in Section 3, was another matter.

2.3 'the helplessness of genteel life'

In writing her various pleas for help, it made sense for Kelly to portray herself as the despairing wife and mother dependent entirely on the kindness of others. In some ways, this self-portrayal was surely accurate: her financial difficulty was real enough, especially as her children grew. The education and future she wanted for them required the help of men and women more wealthy, privileged and influential than herself, and so she had to keep tugging at the heartstrings as a weak, sympathetic victim – a woman who, as she wrote to Hastings, brought to her first marriage nothing but 'a spirit ill suited to my fate, and the helplessness of genteel life' (Kelly 1795a: fol. 93 verso, 94 recto).

It is hard, however, to take Kelly's description of herself to Hastings as entirely convincing. As we've seen, she had already learned in her youth that a woman in her situation could not afford to be *actually* helpless, though she

---

[6] There seems to be no extant copy of this book, but Kelly mentions it in the list of works included in her Royal Literary Fund file, and it was advertised in various periodicals (e.g., 'Education', 1811: 511).

might strategically play that role for others. When she saw her family's financial prospects once again crumble, she once again rose to the challenge. She had been writing poetry since her early teens (Kelly, 1794a: iii), and when the times turned desperate, she turned to her literary abilities as her main resource. Her letter to Hastings in May 1795 provides a snapshot view of that early moment of crisis: while Robert 'in the pride of youth languishes in a prison for £50' (Kelly 1795a: fol. 94 recto), Isabella, left on her own with four-month-old William, tries to find solutions. A note of confidence, perhaps even pride, steals into her words when she writes to Hastings that 'By my pen I have contributed to support my family, and when I finish a work now in hand, I trust with a little assistance to procure him [Robert] liberty' (Kelly, 1795a: fol. 94 recto). This short sentence encapsulates the launching of a literary career that would unfold over decades, and which Kelly managed with determination, resourcefulness and a growing professionalism.

A year after Robert wrote to the Company of 'a wife in a most destitute condition', the wife in question published not only her well-subscribed volume of poetry but the first of her eleven novels, *Madeline, or the Castle of Montgomery* (1794b), which she placed with William Lane's Minerva Press. Lane was fast becoming an obvious address for newcomer women novelists.[7] Publishing her debut novel with him was a natural first step for Kelly, and the beginning of what would prove a nearly decade-long professional alliance. Her first two novels, *Madeline* and *The Abbey of St. Asaph* (1795b), appeared anonymously; starting with the third novel, *The Ruins of Avondale Priory* (1796), she began to sign her name to her fiction, and continued to do so for the rest of her fiction-writing career, with the exception of *Edwardina* (1800), which appeared under the pseudonym of Catherine Harris.

As noted above, by the early 1790s Minerva novels were already being disparaged *en masse*, marked by reviewers as 'separate from even other "low" novels... through a rhetoric that pushed them to the furthest periphery of the genre' (Peiser, 2020: 130), and the contemptuous rhetoric extended to Minerva's authors as well (see Section 1.4). The experiences of the widowed novelist Mrs. Montgomery in *Ruthinglenne*, sneeringly described by another character as 'a poor, pitiful, twopenny-halfpenny writer of trumpery for the circulating libraries' (Kelly, 1801, 3: 181), may tell us something about the indignities involved in being publicly known as a Minerva contributor. Though she likely did not expect to enjoy a very high cultural status as an author, Kelly made a clear effort to raise her profile during her years with

---

[7] Elizabeth Neiman shows that during Minerva's 'zenith' period (1795–1820), the press 'debuts 45 percent of all newcomer female novelists' (Neiman, 2019: 16).

Lane, dedicating novels to distinguished patrons, including the Duchess of York (mentioned above), the Duchess of Gloucester, the Princess of Wales, Lady Louisa Dalling and Lady Anne Culling Smith. Linking herself on title pages to her growing list of novels, she quickly became a Minerva brand name, showcased by Lane in a way that attests to her commercial value to him. In 1798 she was featured prominently in a Minerva publicity prospectus as one of the press's 'particular and favorite authors', alongside Parsons, Roche and seven other women writers (Blakey, 1939: Appendix IV).

During this decade, Kelly also experimented with different ways of increasing her profits. Estimates about how much Lane paid his authors vary, though clearly the pay was fairly low; according to Anthony Mandal, a typical fee for a novel's copyright in this period was around £10 (2014: 163; see also Davies, 2022: 196–202). Kelly was clearly seeking a way to make more money. In addition to dedications and subscription lists, she tried out different publishing arrangements. After placing her first three novels with Lane, presumably by selling the copyright, Kelly had her fourth novel, *Joscelina* (1797), printed privately; a second edition was published by the Minerva Press in 1798 just as Lane published his publicity prospectus, listing *Joscelina* among the Minerva offerings. The following year he published Kelly's *Eva* (1799), and in 1800 he printed *Edwardina* 'for the author' – yet another permutation of his business arrangement with Kelly.

Edwardina, interestingly, also included a 'plug' for Lane: at one point, one of the heroines declares her intention to 'turn Novel writer', noting that 'the Minerva offers liberal encouragement' (Kelly, 1800, 2: 50, 51). As scholars have noted, Lane had a knack for aggressive self-promotion, and it is possible that he encouraged – perhaps even paid for – tributes of this kind inside Minerva novels, a practice that Nicholas Mason calls a 'shameless commingling of the worlds of publicity and literature' (Mason, 2013: 122). If Kelly had arranged to promote Lane in her novel for a profit, she might have felt uneasy about it; that would explain why *Edwardina* is the only one of her novels published under a pseudonym. In any case, her next novel, *Ruthinglenne*, was her last full-fledged Minerva novel. With *The Baron's Daughter* (1802) she moved to John Bell, to whom she had been recommended by her new patron Matthew Lewis (Baron Wilson, 1: 276); perhaps sorry to lose her contributions to his brand, Lane again published a second edition. After that he and Kelly parted ways. *A Modern Incident in Domestic Life* (1803) and *The Secret* (1805a) were published by P. Norbury of Brentford, and *Jane of Dunstanville* (1813), Kelly's last published novel, was again printed privately.

The helplessness and docility of the persona Kelly assumes in her appeals for help are thus complicated by evidence of her assertiveness and initiative in negotiating the literary marketplace. In later years, her resourcefulness showed itself in other ways as well. She published a second edition of her poetry volume (Kelly, 1807) and tried her hand at didactic literature, publishing *The Child's French Grammar* (1805b) and *Instructive Anecdotes for Youth* (1819). She also wrote a memoir of her relative Mrs. Henrietta Fordyce (Kelly, 1823), the widow of Dr. James Fordyce, author of the popular conduct book *Sermons for Young Women* (1766). Embedded in the memoir was yet another self-portrait: Kelly appears in the book as the obliquely named 'Mrs. H——', who – along with her daughter – is invited by Mrs. Fordyce to share her house.

Roger Lonsdale speculates that Kelly 'may have published the memoir partly to make clear to those aware of the situation that she had not simply taken advantage of an elderly woman'(1989: 482). This may well be the case, but the *Memoir of the Late Mrs. Henrietta Fordyce* – which deserves a longer discussion than the present context allows – also offers more evidence of Kelly's talent for covert, fragmented autobiography. Writing it allowed Kelly to tell pieces of her own family story, quoting at length from Mrs. Fordyce's recollections of Elizabeth and William Fordyce's scandalous elopement and of the young Kelly herself, a 'bonny, blithe, blooming lassie, that came jumping before her mother to the Edgeware road' (Kelly, 1823: 89). Through the account of how two widows come to share a house in what she describes as a harmonious and dignified co-existence, Kelly offered a vision of women's life not dominated by hardship and dependency.

This episode in the memoir can thus be seen as a rare divergence from Kelly's 'female drudge' persona – which, unfortunately, she had to assume again a few years later, when (after Mrs. Fordyce's death) she wrote her dismal life story for the gentlemen of the Royal Literary Fund. Even then, however, her resourcefulness remained in evidence: as Colette Davies notes, while submitting her second appeal to the Fund in 1832, Kelly tried to enlist Snow's help in finding a publisher for a book written by her daughter, thus using her contact with the Fund to 'see[k] potential patrons or propitious literary connections' (Davies, 2022: 228). While her letters to the Fund at this late moment in her life offer the same dismal self-portrait she had perfected since her youth – only this time, of a grandmother struggling to support her daughter and grandchildren – once again we can see agency and initiative complicate the familiar image of the suffering drudge.

Kelly, then, spent decades coaxing her experiences into stories that would help her get the help that she needed, and much had to be left out in order for her narratives to serve their purpose. It was in fiction, as the next section will show, that she found a less restrictive domain for telling pieces of her life story – in particular, those pieces which did not fit comfortably within the tale she told to potential patrons. This becomes evident when, equipped with the requisite biographical knowledge, we turn to her first novel, *Madeline, or the Castle of Montgomery* (1794b).

3 Telling Truth in Fiction: *Madeline* (1794)

On its face, *Madeline, or the Castle of Montgomery* would seem to be a run-of-the-mill sentimental novel with the occasional dash of Gothic imagery. Its many tangled storylines converge into the familiar trajectory of sentimental fiction à la Samuel Richardson and Frances Burney, following a young woman who is forced out of her childhood home and into a world of threats. But while she reproduces this familiar narrative structure, Kelly also deviates from it significantly by having Madeline marry her beloved, Arthur Glendillon, midway through the book rather than at the end. This allows her to devote a lengthy portion of the novel to the difficulties of marriage itself – a choice that already hints at how personal experience may have guided her deployment of fictional convention.

Kelly's use of Gothic tropes in *Madeline* is likewise idiosyncratic, and likewise – as this section will show – reflects her private preoccupations. Writing the first of many novels into which she would incorporate Gothic materials in varying dosages (Shapira, 2020b: 172–175), she weaves Gothic elements into the opening of *Madeline* and includes a short, parodic episode set in a crumbling castle in the novel's third volume. Radcliffe seems to be a strong influence: small moments of overlap with *The Mysteries of Udolpho* suggest that Kelly read Radcliffe's best-seller, published in May of 1794, before she finished *Madeline*, which was advertised in July of the same year. (In 1796 she would do the same with Lewis' *The Monk*, responding to it only a few months after its appearance in her own new novel, *The Ruins of Avondale Priory*; see Section 4). Especially given the runaway success of Radcliffe's novel, Kelly's dialogue with it is somewhat puzzling. As I will show in this section, she alters and effectively rejects a particularly successful piece of the Radcliffe formula, while choosing instead to recreate a small scene of *Udolpho* that she might easily have ignored.

While they may seem hard to understand from a commercial perspective, Kelly's choices in handling successful fictional precedents begin to make sense when we view them through the lens of biography. As this section will argue, the central 'tweaks' Kelly makes to the popular formulas of her day align with key experiences in her own life, and in particular – with parts of her life story that were difficult or problematic to tell. When examined vis-à-vis the available biographical facts, *Madeline* proves to be an unacknowledged complement to the 'official' story that Kelly told in her appeals to patrons. It is in the novel, rather than in her requests for help, that she admits to uncomfortable biographical truths, and it is here that we can find the emotions missing from her 'flat', decorous self-portraits. Functioning as a covert form of life writing, her fiction enables her to say what she could not say elsewhere, expressing her disappointment, frustration and rage at the unreliable men on whom her fate depended.

3.1 Elopement and the 'White Gothic'

We can begin to see how Kelly adapts familiar formulas to autobiographical purposes as soon she opens her novel by describing 'the ancient castle of Montgomery' (1794b, 1:1). Like the word 'castle' in Kelly's subtitle, the prompt introduction of a 'gothic piece of architecture' (1: 2) would seem to be a promise of known generic pleasures, indicating that the reader could expect a tale of mystery and fear, perhaps even a suspected ghost or two. That, after all, was the kind of story that writers had unfolded in similar crumbling edifices since Walpole's *The Castle of Otranto*, and the appeal of the formula was only intensified by Radcliffe's skilful and distinctive development of it in *A Sicilian Romance* (1790), *The Romance of the Forest* (1792) and, most recently, *The Mysteries of Udolpho*. If ever there was a piece of Gothic formula worth reproducing for commercial benefit, surely it was the gloomy Gothic castle replete with dangers, especially in the wake of Radcliffe's enormous success.

As Kelly's first few chapters quickly establish, however, the Castle of Montgomery is not that kind of castle. It is not the 'dark opposite' of the ideal home (Ellis, 1989: x); nor is it the setting for thrilling mystery. This castle, rather, is *itself* the home – the ancestral mansion that Madeline's father, Major Montgomery, inherits and lovingly restores with the help of his benevolent, rational wife. Under the Montgomerys' care, the castle is 'fitted up with elegant neatness in the modern taste within, though the outside still preserved its antique grandeur' (1:31). It is also quickly purged of any 'superstition', and thus also of the potential for an eerie Gothic storyline. Scoffing at the servants' rumours of supernatural activity, Mrs. Montgomery fearlessly reclaims the 'haunted' portion of the castle and turns it into a charity school and a 'comfortable asylum for the old and infirm' (Kelly, 1794b, 1: 58). Passing up the opportunity to use the castle as a means of creating pleasurable suspense, Kelly thus turns her Gothic castle into the equivalent of Radcliffe's La Vallée, home of the St. Aubert family, a 'pastoral retreat of bourgeois restraint and discipline' (Miles, 2009: 48).

Why would a first-time Minerva novelist, eager and perhaps desperate to have her work published, reject such a successful fictional precedent? A possible answer to this question emerges when we consider the beginning of *Madeline* through a biographically informed perspective. Kelly repurposes the Gothic castle, I suggest, because in this opening section she is unfolding a version of her own family history; in the story she wishes to tell, the castle has other work to do than its usual function as the menacing 'other' of the modern, normative home.

Although Madeline's parents, Major and Mrs. Montgomery, sound like stock figures of popular fiction, their particular circumstances overlap in several ways with the history of Kelly's parents. Elizabeth Fraser, Kelly's mother, was the niece of Alexander Fraser, Lord Strichen. As their relative Henrietta Fordyce would later tell Kelly, quoting the report she had heard from a Scottish friend, 'bonny Betty F****r' was 'a far and high-descended lassie frae proud Highland clans, with lords and dukes at their heads and tails; and yet she was baith landless and sillerless [pennyless]' (Kelly, 1823: 93, 92). She eloped with 'wild Willy Fordyce' at a ball that she was supposed 'to open... wi' Lord S****n that they were going to marry her to', after which 'the poor things were turned out to the wide world' (93). William secured a commission in the army with the help of a family friend, Lord Adam Gordon, and advanced to the rank of captain (Kelly, 1823: 93).

Much of this detail is repeated in the story of Madeline's parents. Madeline Clifford, the daughter of Lord Clifford, is intended (as Elizabeth Fraser was) for an aristocratic marriage: as a sarcastic bystander tells Archibald, 'her kind papa obliges her to be Lady Rutland with fifteen thousand a year... his lordship taking her without a penny' (Kelly, 1794b 1: 14). The ball at which the Fordyces eloped finds its echo in the ball where Madeline meets Archibald Montgomery, who has a respectable family background but no fortune. They, too, elope and are subsequently cut off. Archibald enters the military with the help of his friend Sir Joseph Cleveland, serving in the West Indies for twenty years and retiring as a major (Kelly, 1794b 1:32).

In the virtuous and principled Montgomerys, then, we can detect Kelly's tribute to her own parents. The Fordyces' history, however, was not entirely compatible with the moralistic conventions of the period's fiction. As Lisa O'Connell describes, elopements were a hotly debated issue in eighteenth-century Britain, especially after the extension of the turnpike network into Scotland in 1770 made it easier for couples to evade the restrictions of the 1753 Hardwicke Marriage Act and cross the border to Gretna Green in Scotland, 'where the old code of consent tolerating clandestine marriage remained in place even after Hardwicke's legislation' (O'Connell, 2019: 190).

In the popular representation of such elopements, the groom 'was usually a dashing adventurer, often a military officer, and his bride-to-be an heiress, love-struck and underage. Angry parents or guardians followed in hot pursuit' (191). This new 'leitmotif of the marriage plot' connected ambitious canonical novels such as Burney's *Camilla* (1796) or Austen's *Pride and Prejudice* (1813) to popular fictions published by the Minerva Press, which, O'Connell claims, 'made the Gretna plot its own', usually in moralistic narratives about 'a young woman's seduction ending in betrayal, unhappiness or death' (202).

Although their location in Scotland rendered a trip to Gretna Green unnecessary, the Fordyces' elopement was still too close for comfort to the stereotypical cautionary tale. Kelly's father was a military officer, her mother the descendant of an illustrious family (though not an heiress), and their marriage left behind a trail of enraged relatives. Kelly seems to have wanted to tell her parents' story in *Madeline*, but she also wanted their fictional alter egos to be embodiments of virtue; having the Montgomerys elope, as her parents had, jeopardized their paragon status. This was the problem she needed to solve, and it was here that the Gothic castle proved useful. By tying the castle to one particular set of ideas associated with 'Gothic', Kelly found a way to cleanse the Montgomerys' marriage of its pejorative connotations and to frame their elopement as being not a moral failure but rather a show of integrity and patriotism.

Unlike his father, a man 'bred in the school of fashion' and given to observing 'with a satirical peevishness, that his ancestors had bequeathed him a heap of ruins', Archibald 'always held the ruins of Montgomery Castle in veneration' (Kelly, 1794b, 1: 4, 7). His kinship to the castle is what ultimately frames and legitimizes his runaway marriage, and to achieve this, Kelly stresses particular aspects of the castle's history: 'erected in those days, when the individual was obliged to preserve himself, and guard his family and property by force of arms' (1: 2), it was given to the Montgomery barons in the eleventh century as a royal reward for their military heroics. Since then it has '[f]or generations... stood the united attacks of war and time' (1: 3). But while the castle has endured as a symbol of self-sufficiency and stamina, the Montgomerys themselves have dwindled in stature as well as wealth – a 'failure of male issue had sunk the title' (1: 3) – while the extravagance of succeeding generations drastically reduced the income from the estate. Only Archibald remains loyal to the castle – and to the values it once represented:

> his mind recoiled from the plodding schemes of the politician... [who] must submit every wish to the plans of state,– must relinquish the darling birthright of a Briton,– freedom... 'No!' cried the noble spirited youth, 'this arm, till nerveless, shall serve the best of sovereigns, but my heart shall still retain its honest freedom ...' (1: 5–6)

Through the kinship she creates between Archibald and the castle, Kelly characterizes both as throwbacks to a glorious and heroic British past – that version of the Middle Ages which Townshend terms 'white Gothic', a 'nostalgic construction of the historical past that is based upon fantasies of chivalry, heroism, and splendour, the liberties enshrined in the Magna Carta, and literal and metaphorical forms of enlightenment' (Townshend, 2019: 33). Archibald's choice of career and wife are thus an expression of the same consecrated British freedom that the 'white Gothic' celebrates, a connection emphasized by the description of both Archibald's father and Lord Clifford, his wife's father, as tyrants (1: 8, 18). The Montgomerys' marriage and subsequent life with their daughters under the '*white* turrets of Montgomery' (2: 80–81, italics added) are thus framed not as shameful filial disobedience but as a show of patriotic independence and integrity. Kelly's opening, then, idealizes her parents' elopement, using the imagery, rhetoric and style of sentimental and Gothic fiction to turn what many must have considered a foolish and damaging act into a show of heroic principle.

Kelly did allow herself greater creative licence in fictionalizing other aspects of the Fordyces' history. For one thing, in crafting the Montgomerys she eliminated her parents' Scottishness, perhaps attesting to the uneasiness displayed even by Scottish writers of Romantic Gothic fiction towards their own nationality and heritage (Wright, 2007: 75–76). As Angela Wright describes, 'Scotland was often referred to as "North Britain" in the periodicals and press of the late eighteenth and early nineteenth centuries' (74), a practice that resonates in Kelly's location of the castle of Montgomery in the 'north of England' (1794b, 1:1). There is clearly something evasive about her choice to make the castle and its occupants inoffensively and broadly 'British'; still, the castle's determined domestication and 'white-Gothic' framing can also be seen as Kelly's covert refusal to treat the north, and, implicitly, Scotland, as 'an uncharted, confusing, and hostile territory' (Wright 74). In a later fictional self-portrait, discussed in Section 3.3, Kelly would openly embrace her Scottish origins.

Kelly also gives Madeline a smaller family than her own: although she notes that Montgomerys had a 'numerous family' (1: 28), she retains for Madeline only one surviving sibling, a younger sister, Ellen. The Montgomerys are also a fantasy version of Kelly's parents in terms of social standing and finances. Although a newspaper clipping from 1848, included in Kelly's Royal Literary Fund file, cites her as saying that she was born in the 'castle… of Caernbro' ('The Mother of Sir Fitzroy Kelly', 1848), there is no reason to think that William Fordyce was supposed to inherit Cairnburgh Castle, or any other family seat. After his discharge, moreover, he still needed the position at court in order to make ends meet, while Major Montgomery retires from the military to a gentlemanly life in at his family estate, with an annual income of £600: 'if my daughters, thought [the Major], are what I wish them, it will be enough, if not, it is too much' (1: 32).

At the beginning of the novel, then, Madeline has reason to expect a comfortable, if not luxurious, future – probably more comfortable than what Kelly and her siblings could have hoped for. But then, in a twist of fate that aligns Madeline with her creator, comes a crisis that alters the family's fortunes, and the heroine's life trajectory with it.

3.2 Men of Feeling

The second and third volumes of Kelly's novel follow Madeline through a variety of challenging situations familiar from other sentimental and Gothic novels, but – again – coloured and inflected by Kelly's personal experiences. In this case, biographical knowledge offers insight into two of the heroine's ordeals – and, indeed, into the fact that these two ordeals are all but identical. In two lengthy episodes that unfold many pages apart, Madeline finds herself facing poverty and danger after the man on whom her well-being depends suffers first a financial breakdown and then an emotional and physical one. In the first episode, this man is her father, Major Montgomery; in the second, it is her husband, Arthur.

Madeline vividly demonstrates Edward Copeland's claim that 'In Minerva Gothic, it is the economy, as it is represented by unpredictable, feckless, improvident, destructive, and tyrannical males, that provides the active source of terror for women' (1995: 41). Masculinity and money combine to become sources of Gothic terror in two different ways: Gothic villains can use their superior strength, freedom and agency to control, withhold or steal money or property from women, à la Radcliffe's Montoni; but they can also terrorize women, albeit unintentionally, through their weakness and ineptitude – a situation which Kelly vividly dramatizes in her novel twice, and which she herself apparently experienced as both a daughter and a wife.

In Archibald Montgomery as Kelly presents him in the opening chapters of *Madeline*, the man of feeling with his 'generous heart' and 'soul replete with all the virtues of humanity' (1: 5) is expanded, through association with the 'white Gothic', into the heroic protector of family, castle and British liberty. The beginning of the second volume, however, severs Archibald from the castle and, appropriately, strips away his heroism, leaving only a particularly fragile version of the hero of sensibility. Major Montgomery, we learn, secretly guaranteed a loan for his friend and neighbour Sir Joseph Cleveland. The latter's speculation leads to catastrophic results, which include not only the loss of the

Clevelands' fortune and Sir Joseph's suicide but the forfeiture of the Montgomery estate as well. The Major is arrested; Mrs. Montgomery collapses and soon dies; when the Major overhears the guards talking of her death, he too falls apart, not only physically but mentally, so that 'Reason was shook on her throne, and his brain became the abode of wild delirium' (2: 45). Later, when the Major is transferred to the King's Bench prison in London, Madeline joins him there to care for him, while her sister Ellen is sent to live with an aunt.

Reading this episode alongside Kelly's poems, it seems clear that the plot twist that sends Madeline on the difficult middle part of her story is modelled after the crisis that scattered Kelly's own nuclear family. While in the preface to her poetry volume Kelly describes her father as a victim, 'injured and oppressed by the unfeeling hand of Power' (Kelly, 1794a: iii–iv), the poems themselves imply that not just external developments but William Fordyce's own weakness left his children destitute and unprotected. In the autobiographical fable 'The Eagle, the Kite and the Cock' (see Section 2.1), the father collapses after the death of the mother, a situation that Kelly describes using virtually the same words she will later use in *Madeline*: the widowed father's 'reason fled' and, although his children try to revive him, a 'wild delirium still prevail'd' (1794a: 64). By the time he comes to his senses, his position at court is lost, and he helplessly turns to his daughter for assistance. In another poem, 'The Vision', 'William' remains inconsolable after the death of 'Eliza'. Wandering at night and lamenting his loss, he sees the ghost of his dead wife, who reassures him that she is in a happier place – but also urges him to 'protect our race, / 'Tis thine to guide their youth' (1794a: 46). The grieving William Fordyce may, too, have needed reminding of his paternal responsibilities, and the fate of the scattered chicks in 'The Eagle, the Kite and the Cock' suggests that such a reminder did not arrive in time.

In Archibald Montgomery, I want to suggest, Kelly begins to grapple with a theme that had strong resonance within her own life, and which would continue to run through her later fiction as well: male weakness and its implications for women (see Shapira, 2020b). While elsewhere in her fiction she would imagine men succumbing to various external threats – war, illness, criminal violence – her particular emphasis in *Madeline* is on men who collapse under the weight of their own feelings. Significantly, it is in the context of exploring this propensity that she makes her most distinct nod to *The Mysteries of Udolpho*, although the moment in Radcliffe's novel that Kelly chooses to echo would seem at first to involve the dangers of *female* emotion. After her mother dies, Emily is cautioned by her father against 'the indulgence of excessive grief': sorrow, St. Aubert claims, 'becomes a selfish and unjust passion, if indulged at the expence of our duties – by our duties I mean what we owe to ourselves, as well as to others' (Radcliffe, 1998: 20). Kelly offers her own version of this conversation, with two important differences. First, since the Major is incapacitated after his wife's death, it is the kindly local clergyman who urges Madeline and Ellen to 'indulge not fruitless grief... and thereby render yourselves unfit to offer dutiful attention to your sole surviving parent' (2: 47). Secondly, what St. Aubert describes as one's broader 'duties' towards oneself and others narrows, in *Madeline*, into a single task: that of caring for the Major.

Kelly's variation on Radcliffe thus clearly establishes that the Major's suffering has emptied out his paternal function, leaving him dependent on his daughters' strength. But is this, in fact, such a sharp deviation from Radcliffe? As Claudia Johnson has argued, the perils of male sensibility are already evoked in *The Mysteries of Udolpho*, albeit in a far subtler form. St. Aubert's gentle admonition of Emily for her grief comes just minutes after he himself struggles to read the evening prayer, during which 'his voice often faltered, [and] his tears fell upon the book' (20). This muted acknowledgement of St. Aubert's emotional susceptibility is later extended in the narrator's explanation of his subsequent illness: 'His constitution had never recovered from the late attack of the fever, and the succeeding shock it received from Madame St. Aubert's death had produced its present infirmity' (25). If we are paying close attention, we might recognize that what ultimately causes Emily's troubles is not her own sensibility but rather her father's, which the novel quietly glosses over while making *her* emotions the focus of didactic attention: 'We may be enabled to critique this recurrent discrepancy [between standards for emotion in men and women]', Johnson writes, 'but we are not encouraged to do so' (1995: 101).

What, we might wonder, was it like for a woman to read *The Mysteries of Udolpho* after first losing her mother and then seeing her father collapse into his own grief? Might such a reader have noted St. Aubert's over-emotionality, despite the novel's overt focus on the perils of *female* sensibility? And if that woman were to write a novel of her own in the sentimental/Gothic vein, what kind of father would she choose to give her heroine? *Madeline* provides two answers to the latter question. Kelly writes Archibald Montgomery first by aggrandizing a recognizable version of William Fordyce into a 'white-Gothic' hero. But then, as she describes the crisis which sets the heroine's ordeals in motion, she writes the father again as a different kind of popular stereotype, the man of feeling; and for all the rhetoric praising the Major for his fine qualities and deep feelings, the novel also allows us to see clearly that his sensibility is what puts his wife and daughters in danger.

The Major's strong sense of friendship and gratitude towards his friend Sir Joseph, whom he beheld 'as something more than mortal' (2: 102), leads him to sign the 'fatal paper' (2: 110) that makes him liable for Sir Joseph's debts. When describing the Major's reaction to his arrest and his wife's death, Kelly abandons any subtlety, her language itself coloured by Archibald's hysteria: he is depicted as 'frantic', filled with 'unexpected frenzy', 'his senses sunk in unconscious stupor' (2: 29, 43, 38). This portrayal emphasizes precisely what *The Mysteries of Udolpho* downplays: that a man's sensibility and frailty is the real cause of the heroine's suffering, since his breakdown in the face of hardship means the collapse of the order that was supposed to protect her.

Kelly's focus on male emotion as the real chink in the family armour becomes clearer through repetition, as the same liability recurs when Madeline and her husband, Arthur, find themselves in financial crisis. Arthur is not as clearly tied to Robert Kelly as Major Montgomery is to William Fordyce, since Kelly gives him few identifying characteristics: we know only that he is a younger son dependent on the fortune of his uncle, and that he possesses the qualities – graceful figure, exalted virtues, refined sentiments – required of a hero of sensibility (2: 226). It is suggestive, however, that 'Arthur' is also the name Kelly uses in her poems for the lover or husband of her speaker, usually called 'Anna', and here the connection to Robert becomes stronger. The poetic Arthur, like the fictional one, seems for the most part a standard romance figure; but the poem 'To Arthur' does characterize him as a military man, whom 'Anna' vows to support 'should again thy country claim thine arm, / To guard our rights, or shield our land from harm' (Kelly, 1794a: 17). If the 'Arthur' of the poems was Kelly's version of Robert, there is reason to think she had occasion to worry about her husband's moods. In 'On Beholding Arthur Sleep', the speaker mentions her 'anxious mind' and expresses her intention to 'fondly watch' over his sleep or, when he wakes, to 'charm his soul to rest' (1794a: 48). 'Anna' is again tasked with cheering a discontented mate in 'Extempore on Arriving in the Country', where she wonders whether her 'care', 'tenderness' and 'anxious love' can keep her beloved from resenting the 'languor of a solitary scene' (1794a: 33).

The autobiographical resonance of Arthur as a stand-in for Robert Kelly grows clearer when Madeline and Arthur suddenly find themselves in financial trouble, as the Kellys did in the wake of the Colonel's death. After reading the bankruptcy reports in the morning paper, Madeline immediately recognizes that her husband's reaction will be crucial to what happens next. Reluctant to share the news with him, she finally prefaces the revelation with a plea: 'Be then yourself, my Arthur, and I am happy – be resigned, and I am calm' (3: 128). In the days and weeks that follow, while the Glendillons both face the same grim reality, Arthur mostly feels, and Madeline – though filled with emotions of her own – resolutely acts. It is she who finds the family cheaper accommodations, sells off valuables and takes in embroidery work (as she had done while her father was incarcerated). When an unpaid bill finally sends Arthur to prison, Madeline draws strength from her own previous experiences: 'She had been often in a prison – and the horror of bolts, gates, and hard unfeeling faces had greatly lost their effect – and beside, she repressed her emotions, and assumed the heroine, to inspire her husband with resolution, and give him comfort' (3: 146). But however well Madeline 'assumes the heroine', it is not enough to lift Arthur out of his despondency. While 'in the presence of his wife', the narrator reveals, he 'wore an air of serenity... when alone he gave way to all the emotions of misery and despair', and his state of mind eventually becomes a physical malaise. As Madeleine anxiously notes, 'an alarming languor appeared fast gaining on the sensible mind of her husband, and a slow fever weaken[ed] his constitution', until he falls dangerously ill (3: 134, 148).

There are no surviving documents to tell us how Robert reacted to the change in his circumstances, beyond his desperate petition to the East India Company (R. H. Kelly, 1793) and the one telling line in Kelly's letter to Hastings, where she claims that her husband 'in the pride of youth languishes in a prison for £50' (Kelly 1795a: fol. 94 recto). If we add this line to the various poems focused on a woman's efforts to manage the moods of an unhappy man and to Kelly's frenzied efforts to make money from the mid 1790s on, it seems likely that the fictional crisis in *Madeline* draws heavily on Kelly's own experience.

Kelly's resolution of this crisis, moreover, can be seen as a fantasy ending to her own troubles, written when those troubles were still very much unrelieved in real life: generous friends step in, and Madeline and Arthur are restored to wealth, health and marital happiness. Tellingly, though, the various solutions that materialize have little to do with Arthur and everything to do with his wife. It is Madeline's valiant effort that saves her husband's life (she pawns her wedding ring to buy him medicine), and it is her past kindnesses to others that are repaid in the help they now receive. It also cannot be a coincidence that part of the fantasy Kelly spins involves Arthur's willingness to accept help. When a wealthy family friend proposes to support them through the crisis, Madeline looks uneasily at her husband: 'His ambition was independence – but pride alone could have refused the bounty', and Arthur agrees to the offer and 'felt not humbled' by it (3: 183–184). Writing her novel in 1794, Kelly was probably hoping that Robert, like Arthur, would save his family from further suffering by recognizing his own limitations and accepting the support and patronage of wealthier friends. She did not yet know that the happy ending she dreamed up for her heroine was not one that she would experience for herself.

3.3 A Tale of Two Madelines

Here is one final curious fact about *Madeline*: seven years after she published it, Kelly recycled Madeline Montgomery. By this, I do not mean that she wrote new adventures for her first heroine, who presumably remained where Kelly left her in 1794, living happily ever after with Arthur in the castle. Rather, Kelly gave Madeline's name to a new character, a widow who appears halfway through her 1801 novel *Ruthinglenne* to help the young heroine, Benigna, at a crucial moment in her ongoing ordeals. This Madeline Montgomery does not come from a vaguely defined 'north of England' but is rather 'descended from some of the highest and the proudest of the Scottish clans' (Kelly, 1801, 2: 244). Her husband, Charles, is not a standard-issue hero of sensibility but an army captain of limited means but 'brilliant' prospects, thanks to an expected inheritance from his father, a high-ranking commander in India (2: 245). But then General Montgomery dies – in a duel, of all things – and the money is lost. Struggling to make ends meet, Madeline finds paid work for herself – not as an embroiderer but as a novelist.

As all this detail should make clear, in 1801 Kelly decided to write herself into *Ruthinglenne* far more explicitly than she had in *Madeline*, creating an alter ego laden with specifics from her own biography. Her decision to repeat Madeline Montgomery's name invites us to read the two heroines side by side, as two different composites of fact and fiction that Kelly created at two different moments in her life and career. As we have seen, the history of the first Madeline mirrored aspects of Kelly's complicated feelings towards her father and her husband. In that early novel, however, Kelly had relied on the license of fiction-writing and on the idealizing potential of sentimental and Gothic conventions to soften, beautify and resolve what in real life probably stayed painful and messy to the end. But by the time she wrote *Ruthinglenne*, Kelly had lost some of her restraint. She used the second Madeline Montgomery to tell an angrier, uglier story about the men who had failed her, this time placing her husband, Robert, front and centre.

Glossing quickly over the childhood of the second Madeline, Kelly describes how, as a young woman '[b]red to elegance, in the bosom of parental tenderness', she found herself destitute and alone at the age of eighteen (2: 244). The formative event of this Madeline's life involves not her parents but the man she marries: 'Fortune, or Misfortune, introduced her to Captain Montgomery' (2: 245). As she did throughout her life (see Section 2.2), Kelly refused even in fiction to admit that her husband had been disowned by his father; there is no falling-out between Charles and General Montgomery, who 'entirely approved of his son's union' and left Charles £20,000 in his will (2: 245). Yet the money still mysteriously disappears, and Charles and Madeline learn only that 'the General, some months before his death, had withdrawn all his property; and how disposed of it was unknown, but he died insolvent' (2: 246).

Although she maintains her silence on what caused Robert to lose his fortune, Kelly abandons her previous reserve when it comes to portraying his reaction to the loss. The story of Madeline and Charles is a frank, angry indictment of a man's irresponsibility towards his family and disrespect towards his wife and their friends. The Montgomerys, Kelly suggests, could have extricated themselves from their difficulties: 'Youth, mutual affection, buoyant spirits, and high connections, in a little time might have surmounted the evil; and such was the interest their talents, loveliness, and misfortunes excited, that independence would have been their own in a supereminent degree' (2: 246). It is not enough, however, to have patronage available. One needs to cultivate, use and protect it, and this is where Charles utterly fails, as 'those friends the shining qualities of Captain Montgomery acquired, his haughty, inconsiderate, volatile nature lost' (2: 246). He not only manages to alienate his benefactors but behaves recklessly with what little money he has, 'till improvidence at home, and dissipated profuseness abroad, reduced the family to the lowest ebb of human wretchedness'. Madeline begins to write for money while trying desperately to hold on to their patrons: she 'concealed and justified, justified and concealed, the imprudences of him she loved, till the generous few who patronized her, and aided her struggles, implicated her in his follies, and one by one dropped off' (2: 247).

Through the florid language Kelly usually employs to describe marriage, we nonetheless read the painful story of a couple whose relationship deteriorates along with their finances – the story, it seems likely, of Kelly's own marriage to Robert. Madeline implores Charles to change his ways, but their exchanges inevitably end 'with haughty anger on one side and silent anguish on the other' (2: 247). To his '[f]rigid indifference' and 'haughty reserve', Charles eventually adds the devastating insult of adultery: 'the bosom she had selected as a refuge from every storm... rejected the tender claims, and sacrificed its energy at the shrine of another' (2: 248–249). Under such strain, Kelly acknowledges, the feelings of even the most devoted wife can change. Madeline's 'delighted duty' towards her husband, 'so long the offspring of tenderness, at length became the cold result of principle', and because 'the fervid heart *must* have some object to bestow its fervor on', she 'gave to the children what no longer interested the father' (2: 249).

The 'pride of youth' that, as Kelly wrote to Hastings in 1795, kept Robert in prison for a debt of £50 (Kelly, 1795a: fol. 94 recto) is evident as well in the case of Charles Montgomery. After he is arrested at a 'noted gaming house' (2: 249), the '[h]aughty and unbending' Charles feels no remorse or concern for his family; or if he does, Kelly comments, any such feeling 'faded where it rose, in the deep recesses of a wounded spirit. Days, weeks, months elapsed; still he lingered in prison – still his wife endured the extremest anguish, difficulty, and reproach' (2: 249–250). Reprising the events of *Madeline* in a different key, Kelly leads Charles to a decidedly different end from Arthur's. A fever breaks out in the prison, and Charles dies. Instead of obtaining the medicine that leads to her husband's miraculous recovery, this Madeline comes to the prison to weep over his corpse.

Robert is not the only target of Kelly's veiled exposé in *Ruthinglenne*. The character of a former British commander in India, a friend of the late General Montgomery, suggests that Kelly may also have been settling a score with Hastings: his putative fictional counterpart, 'Colonel Grambold', rudely rebuffs Madeline's request for help, a humiliating experience that Kelly describes in much poignant detail before turning Grambold into a Gothic villain (see Shapira, 2022 for a full discussion). As she had done in the two bird fables in her poems, Kelly in *Ruthinglenne* thus resumes her role as secret historian, using the guise of fiction express her grievances against those more powerful than herself, to assert her own virtue and integrity, and to solicit sympathy and support.

The Montgomerys' foundation in fact would have been evident to any reader familiar with the Kellys, and such a readers were, indeed, available: although *Ruthinglenne* was intended for Lane's usual library patrons, who would have had no idea that Kelly was writing about herself, the novel's list of subscribers suggests a more immediate and knowing circle of addressees. Kelly dedicated *Ruthinglenne* to Lady Louisa Dalling, the widow of General Sir John Dalling, who commanded the British forces in Madras during the years when Robert and his father were stationed there. The list of subscribers that Lady Dalling helped Kelly to assemble includes many people with ties to the East India Company (see Shapira, 2022: 127–130). For this small subset of the reading audience, Kelly's fictionalization of her experience was not really meant to conceal; rather, it was a covert but legible way for Kelly to appeal directly to a circle of potential patrons, dissociating herself from Robert's misdeeds and expressing her continued need for help and connections.

As I have tried to show in this section, reading formula fiction and biography together allows them to illuminate and deepen one another. Biographical knowledge allows us to detect the particular, personally significant use that Kelly makes of novelistic conventions in *Madeline* and *Ruthinglenne*. At the same time, recognizing what Kelly does with her own experience in *Madeline* and *Ruthinglenne* allows us to see a fuller picture of her at two key moments of her life. Less through its contents than by its very nature, *Madeline* introduces us to the thirty-five-year-old woman who, after her family's finances suffered a devastating blow, mobilized her literary ability into a source of income while her husband withdrew into his hurt pride. Not satisfied with quickly writing a publishable work of fiction, she used her first novel to pay tribute to her parents – and perhaps also to process the unsettling experience of having watched her father's authority and resilience crumble. She also began to write, as she would continue to do, of the enormous uncertainty that opened up in a woman's life when the man she loved proved less durable than herself. Through the lines of *Ruthinglenne* we glimpse the same woman a few years later: now forty-one years old, a mother of three and an established popular novelist, she decides to start telling the truth about her husband, still carefully combining fact and fiction as she vents her rage and courts new patrons.

Freed from the limited range of poses she assumes in her petitions for help, the Kelly we glimpse in these novels is a woman endowed with a full range of human emotions, including anger and hurt at Robert's betrayal, and humiliation and resentment for what seems to have been Hastings' indifference. She is also a canny and calculating agent in her own life story – a novelist who, despite the limits on self-expression imposed by her gender, class and financial situation, nevertheless finds ways to speak her mind and, moreover, uses her fiction to signal precisely what kind of help she requires.

It is surely no coincidence that of all the kindnesses paid to Madeline Montgomery at the end of *Ruthinglenne*, none is praised as highly as the offer made by one of the novel's aristocrats to become a patron to Madeline's oldest son. No act, Kelly's narrator claims, is 'more approved by the God of perfect goodness, than that of sustaining and instructing the child of innocence and misfortune' (Kelly, 1801, 3: 159). Through her fictional alter ego, Kelly spelled out what she most needed – and the need was shortly afterwards met by her new benefactor, Matthew Lewis. His relationship with Kelly and what we might learn from it about Kelly and, more broadly, about the trade–canon dialogue will be the subject of the final section.

4 Kelly and Lewis: The Prequel

According to his first biographer, Margaret Baron Wilson, Matthew Lewis was introduced to Kelly by a bookseller after an 'incident – somewhat similar to one occurring in the "Castle Spectre"' appeared in one of her novels (1: 270). He was moved by her difficulties and tried to help her, making inquiries about money owed to her father at the War Office and, when this effort failed, offering to pay for William's education. He also gave Kelly professional advice and introduced her to his publisher, Joseph Bell. His brief professional patronage of her ended abruptly in 1803, after a newspaper advertisement announced that Lewis was helping Kelly with a novel. Kelly had praised Lewis, indirectly but lavishly, in *A Modern Incident in Domestic Life* (1803), and Lewis feared that people would think he had 'written [his] own praises' (Baron Wilson 1: 279). He nonetheless continued to support William until the latter's profligacy soured their relationship; he and Kelly apparently remained on good terms.

With the exception of Montague Summers' (1964: 263–267) long-debunked claim that William Kelly and Matthew Lewis were lovers, the story I have just summarized has changed little over the years (see Baron Wilson, 1839: 270–281; Peck, 1961: 62–66; D. L. Macdonald, 2000: 60–63; Townshend, 2024: 30–33). Based almost entirely on Lewis' letters, it offers a lucid demonstration of how Kelly has been 'flattened' by the very documents that preserve information about her life. All we can see from the letters is Lewis' side of the relationship; Kelly is present only in her statements to Lewis as he recorded them, and these are predictably bland and deferential. When the advertisement announcing their collaboration appeared in the newspaper, Kelly (according to Lewis) reassured him that she did not have 'the least idea how [it] came to be inserted, and that she was very unhappy at its having appeared' (Baron Wilson, 1839: 275). After Lewis' own straitened finances caused him to stop supporting William, she sent him what he called 'a very kind answer (rather too enthusiastic, indeed)' (1: 308). 'Poor Mrs. K[elly]' also told him, as he wrote, that being a novelist was an 'odious task', at which she only persisted to support her children (1: 277, 278). Since Kelly did not leave behind an archive of her own, we have no other source of information about their relationship, and thus no way of knowing how Kelly saw it. If she had any feelings, ambitions, thoughts and plans that did not fit her role as the grateful object of Lewis' charity, these never made it into his letters; Kelly herself would have been careful not to reveal them.

Lewis' correspondence thus contributes to the cumulative 'flattening' of Kelly's persona by her various appeals to patrons. But the story we have of their personal relationship also has bigger implications. In the tale of the assertive, active canonical author and his grateful, unambitious protégée we can see, personified, the common view of canonical Gothic and trade Gothic. As Lewis and Kelly's story seems to confirm, the canon–trade relationship is fundamentally unequal and hierarchical: complexity, agency, originality and ability are only ever found on one side, and influence only ever flows in one direction.

In this section I aim to complicate the familiar tale of patronage and dependency on both the personal and the literary-historical level by showing that, much like the trade–canon dialogue, Kelly's relationship with Matthew Lewis was more complicated than it has seemed. I will make this case using the one source with which Lewis' biographers have never been familiar: Kelly's novels, particularly those novels she published before she and Lewis became personally acquainted. Offering a kind of 'prequel' to the familiar story, I use Kelly's novels in this section to trace her path towards the personal acquaintance she struck up with Lewis. This path passed from the early days of her own career, which preceded Lewis' literary debut, through her complex reaction to his fiction and drama, to the moment when they actually met.

The Kelly that emerges from this previously unrecognized part of the story is neither a supplicant nor a hack: she is a novelist with artistic preferences that she began to develop before ever reading a word that Lewis wrote. She is also a participant – like Lewis himself – in the rich play of borrowing and revising that characterized the Gothic–Romantic moment. And although Kelly was clearly stimulated by the powerful example of *The Monk* and *The Castle Spectre* (1797), the novels she published after Lewis appeared on the literary scene suggests that she retained her own sense of preference and direction, reacting to Lewis with a mixture of admiration, resistance and creative revision.

4.1 Kelly before Lewis (1795): Theatrical Hauntings

Kelly's 1795 novel *The Abbey of St. Asaph* contains a lively experiment in the type of spectacular 'horror Gothic' that would later become synonymous with Lewis – an experiment conducted, significantly, while Lewis himself was still unknown. The Gothic portion of the novel sends young Jennet to the eponymous abbey in Wales, founded by the family's famed ancestor, Owen of Trevallion; not far from the abbey is an ancient castle, whose ruins are now said to be haunted. The owner of the abbey, Sir Hugh, inherited the estate after the sudden death of his older brother, Sir Eldred, whose infant daughter mysteriously vanished. Jennet eventually discovers that Sir Eldred is alive in the abbey dungeons and that she, of course, is his daughter, the lost heiress of St. Asaph. Radcliffe's influence remains in evidence in Kelly's second novel, and it is indeed not hard to understand why a reviewer described *The Abbey of St. Asaph* as having been written in 'humble imitation of the well-known novels of Mrs. Radcliffe' ('Novels and Romances', 1795: 349). But even as she offers readers a pleasurable walk down a familiar Radcliffean path, Kelly begins to break away stylistically in a direction of her own, foreshadowing Lewis' more famous departures from Radcliffe's example a year later in *The Monk*.

In the familiar account of Gothic literary history, Radcliffe and Lewis represented two divergent approaches to the writing of Gothic, with Radcliffe seeking the subtle effect of terror and Lewis cultivating the blunter one of horror. Where Radcliffe expertly threw light and shadows around threats that were left partly hidden from both her heroines and her readers, Lewis depicted the sources of fear and horror in vivid, graphic detail. Kelly's handling of a scene set in the abbey's burial vault initially suggests that she is adopting Radcliffe's terror-oriented technique: following Jennet as she descends to the vault, the narrator describes how 'small apertures in the roof, which admitted faint gleams of light' add 'inconceivable horror' to the 'rugged cavern' (Kelly 1795b 3: 11). The mixture of darkness and intermittent light is a nod to the burial vault beneath the Castle of Udolpho, where Emily's imagination is stirred to terror by the isolated gleams that interrupt the 'general obscurity' (Radcliffe, 1998: 378). Eventually, however, Kelly abandons the subtleties of terror to describe the horrors of the vault, with its 'bodies... in different stages of decay' and 'mouldering bones' (Kelly, 1795b, 3: 12). Horrified, Jennet flees, convinced that she is doomed to pass her 'few remaining hours... breath[ing] the vapid air of corruption' (3:13). A reader familiar with *The Monk* might well be reminded here of Agnes in the vault of St. Clare's Convent, surrounded by 'loathsome and mouldering Bodies' and a 'noisome suffocating smell' (Lewis, 1995: 403). Agnes, however, existed in 1795 only in the draft of the novel that Lewis was possibly circulating to friends but had not yet published (Townshend, 2024: 17).

Kelly anticipates Lewis in more than just a fondness for macabre detail. There is a kind of gleeful inventiveness to her portrayal of the strange sights Jennet encounters, a decidedly un-Radcliffean lingering on the stimulus rather than the response. Strolling through the castle ruins, Jennet comes across a series of strange occurrences:

> ... a rolling noise, sounding like distant thunder, issued from the earth, and shook the place beneath her.
> The moon was suddenly obscured in deep and awful darkness ... and a mighty wind, rushing thro' the hollow caverns with howling blasts, shook the ancient fabric to the foundation.
> A heavy bell tolled with deep and solemn sound, and the most terrific shrieks, and lamentable groans, burst from the subterranean cavities of the building.
> ... [The] still-agitated earth ... opened wide before her, when a figure ascended, which slow and gradual rose to a stupendous height ... The head was large, and almost shapeless; something like a countenance appeared in front, but horrible beyond imagination; the eyes seemed globes of fire; and the gaping jaws emitted sulphurous flames; the bristled hair stood erect, and a vesture which floated loosely around the spectre, represented by pale gleams of light, the forms of every noxious reptile. (2: 221–223)

Identifying itself as the ghost of Sir Owen, the figure warns Jennet to stay away from the castle ruins before sinking back into the ground.

The same creativity in designing vivid Gothic stimuli is evident later in the vault scene, when Jennet, hearing a strange noise,

> looked wildly round, and beheld a human skeleton on the earth before her: Not a fibre remained – yet the bare ribs shook, – the ghastly skull rose slow, yet visible, to view; and disconsolately bowing, seemed to implore commiseration. Something glistened within the hollow sockets, which once inclosed the orbs of sight, and a faint shriek issued from the yawning jaws.

> ... A deep sigh penetrated her ear, – piteous moans succeeded; which sinking in undistinguishable sound, – an anthem, softly melancholy, was heard in a low plaintive voice. She was listening to the soothing accents with pleasing wonder, when the skull, parting from the neck, with shrill shrieks, rolled to her foot. (3: 13–14, 14–15)

Vivid and material, Kelly's two 'ghost' scenes in *The Abbey of St. Asaph* anticipate Lewis in more than just their bluntness. The attention Kelly lavishes on spectacle at these moments suggests that she shared with Lewis a theatrical sensibility and a particular interest in the potential of Gothic stage spectacle. As Lewis would soon do as well in *The Monk*, Kelly in these scenes mimics in verbal description what the dramatists of the day were doing on the London stage.

As has been widely discussed, Gothic drama from the 1790s on took 'full advantage of advances in lighting, machinery and staging to offer overwhelming sets and supernatural special effects' (Cox, 2001: 110). Lewis would become the unrivalled master of such spectacles; his most famous precursor was James Boaden, who based his *Fontainville Forest* (1794) on Radcliffe's *The Romance of the Forest* (1791). Deciding to abandon Radcliffe's 'explained supernatural', Boaden displayed the ghost of Adeline's father onstage in a carefully engineered feat of stagecraft. One actor delivered the ghost's lines from the wings in a 'hollow voice', while another actor, chosen for his 'tall, sweeping figure', moved silently across the stage, a backlit screen of blue-grey gauze making him seem to 'floa[t]... like a shadow' (Boaden, 1824, 2: 119, 118, 119). Boaden also exploited other innovative possibilities of set construction and special effects, opening the fourth act with 'Violent Thunder and Light'ning, the Abbey rocks, and through the distant Windows one of the Turrets is seen to fall, struck by Light'ning' (Boaden, 1794: 41). As Bertram Evans notes, 'This setting, with its combination of spectacular sounds and action, is a striking beginning of the catastrophic pictures which, after Boaden's play, were staged with increasing violence.... Carpenters and painters were kept busy preparing scenery that would rise, sink, fall, explode, or otherwise create startling effects' (2020: 100–101).

In 1794 and early 1795, as Kelly was writing *The Abbey of St. Asaph*, Covent Garden presented three Radcliffe adaptations (Evans 2020: 91): in addition to Boaden's *Fontainville Forest* (March 1794), audiences could also enjoy Henry Siddons' *The Sicilian Romance: or, The Apparition of the Cliffs* (May 1794) and Miles Peter Andrews' *The Mysteries of the Castle* (January 1795). There is no way to know whether Kelly had the time or means to go to the theatre. But even if she did not attend the performances, she would likely have read or heard about them, and she seems to have been deeply attuned to the working of stage spectacle. Since she opts in this novel to give naturalistic explanations to seemingly supernatural events (another Radcliffean strategy that she would abandon in some of her later works), her 'ghost' scenes are literally about the potential of theatrical expertise. When the ghosts are explained away, what we are left with are various manmade techniques for creating powerful illusions.

As we later learn, Sir Hugh inherited the abbey by ordering his physician-henchman, Doctor Martin, to kill his older brother, Sir Eldred. The doctor, however, took pity on Sir Eldred, who has since been a secret prisoner. To convince Sir Hugh that his brother was dead, Doctor Martin removed the corpse of the two brothers' father from its tomb, smeared it with blood and presented it to Sir Hugh as evidence. Jennet is frightened in the vault by the skeletal remains of that first gruesome display, enhanced by a random natural occurrence: what causes the skeleton to move and shriek is not an unquiet spirit but a 'monstrous overgrown rat' sheltering inside it (Kelly, 1795b, 3: 128). Having apparently developed his skill for spectacle-making over the years, Doctor Martin later also staged the appearance of Sir Owen's fiery 'ghost' in order to scare away Jennet and Sir Hugh, both of whom had taken to wandering the castle ruins. In a meticulously designed performance, Doctor Martin rose up through 'well known trap doors' after having 'assumed a horrible appearance' with the help of 'a chemical preparation of phosphorus', thus combining what in the theatre would be costuming, machinery and special effects (3: 94, 93). And although Doctor Martin does not explain its provenance, the 'vesture' on which 'gleams of light' (2: 223) cast frightening figures sounds remarkably like the magic-lantern shows and more recent 'phantasmagoria' performances, which used evolving projection technologies to entertain viewers with macabre images (see Jones, 2021).

Just two years later, Matthew Lewis would create one of the period's most powerful and popular Gothic spectacles, that of Evelina's ghost in *The Castle Spectre* – a combination of staging, costuming, lighting and music orchestrated to maximize the impact of the spectral figure at its centre. Already in *The Monk*, however, we can see him writing the supernatural as a combination of theatrical elements, just as Kelly had done in *The Abbey of St. Asaph*. Matilda's summoning of the demon in the convent vault, in fact, bears a striking resemblance to the scene in which Jennet sees Owen de Trevallion's 'ghost'. Kelly combines a backdrop of 'Gothic arches... in magnificent decay' (2: 218) with shaking ground, strange groans and the sound of 'a mighty wind, rushing thro' the hollow caverns with howling blasts' (2: 222), setting the stage for the appearance of the phosphorescent ghost, clad in the 'vesture' on which 'pale gleams of light' created 'the forms of every noxious reptile' (2: 223). Lewis, for his part, invents 'a spacious Cavern' in which a 'blast... howled along the lonely Vaults'

(Lewis 1995: 275) and adds music as well as pyrotechnics and special effects – 'a pale sulphurous flame arose from the ground' (275); 'the ground shook beneath the feet of the Enchantress' (276). All these converge around the spectacular figure that suddenly manifests in the vault, a naked youth whose head is surrounded by 'many-coloured fires' that 'for[m] themselves into a variety of figures' (277), rather like the forms cast by light on Sir Owen's 'vesture'.

It is extremely tempting at this moment to wonder whether Lewis might have read *The Abbey of St. Asaph* and found inspiration in it. But there is no direct evidence to support this suggestion; moreover, *The Monk* was likely already written when *The Abbey of St. Asaph* came out, and both Lewis and Kelly were working with formulaic materials. Leaving the notion of trade-to-canon influence for now as an intriguing speculation to which I will return in my conclusion, I will settle for arguing that Kelly and Lewis, unbeknownst to each other, were indulging similar predilections in their writing of this period. The kinship between them would likely have been evident to Kelly when, the following year, she read a new novel by a still-unnamed author: *The Monk*.

4.2 Kelly after Lewis (1799–1800): Repurposed Female Ghosts

Based on certain details in the plot of her third novel, *The Ruins of Avondale Priory* (1796), it seems very likely that Kelly read *The Monk* shortly after its initial publication. Her heroine, Ethelinde, at one point finds herself in exactly the same predicament as Lewis' Antonia: she is drugged into a state of seeming death and brought to a monastic burial vault by a lustful man. Even if we take Kelly and Lewis' shared preferences into account, the overlap is too specific to seem accidental. *The Monk* came out in March 1796; *The Ruins of Avondale Priory* was advertised as published in July. Kelly was probably still finishing her novel when she read *The Monk*, and Lewis' impact is evident in various ways in *The Ruins of Avondale Priory*, including a queer episode that acknowledges, but also revises, the queerness of Lewis' book (see Shapira, 2020c).

It must have been exciting for Kelly to see her own nascent predilections as a Gothic writer mirrored back to her with so much force and talent, and she reacted to the experience with an intriguing mix of admiration and resistance. The fact that she chose to engage with *The Monk* so soon after its appearance suggests the strength of her personal reaction to it, since she could not have been seeking the commercial advantage of belonging to the 'Lewis school'; there was not yet any such school to belong to. Published anonymously, *The Monk* initially received only a short reviews; only after the second edition of September 1796, signed 'M.G. Lewis, Esq., M.P.', did the book became a public scandal and a sensation, by which point *The Ruins of Avondale Priory* had been out for months. Kelly's choice to adapt pieces of *The Monk* while it was still relatively obscure tells us that she found it enjoyable, perhaps even galvanizing; and indeed, her dialogue with it would continue for years to come.

Judging by Kelly's writing after *The Monk*, one particular piece especially appealed to her imagination: in both *Eva* (1799) and *Edwardina* (1800), characters find themselves face to face with a mysterious veiled woman who fills them with terror and awe. Few readers of the day could have failed to recognize the resemblance of this figure to Lewis' most famous creations: the Bleeding Nun in *The Monk*, joined a year later onstage by the ghost of Evelina in *The Castle Spectre*.

Before looking at what Kelly did with these figures, it is important to stress just how unstable the concept of originality becomes in this context. Both of Lewis' ghosts were themselves amalgams of varied source materials, to which Lewis added his own innovations and emphases. As Lewis himself acknowledged (1995: 6), the Bleeding Nun was drawn from German folk traditions, although contemporaries claimed that he had plagiarized more recent print sources (see Townshend, 2024: 124–131); Gottfried August Bürger's 'Lenore', whose first English translations appeared in early 1796, is another clear influence (Milbank, 2009: 80). In designing the appearance of Evelina in *The Castle Spectre*, Lewis opted for a somewhat different kind of spectre, eerie and poignant rather than gruesome: dressed in 'white and flowing garments spotted with blood', she throws back her veil to reveal a 'pale and melancholy countenance' (Lewis, 1798: 79). This ghost, too, had its precursors. Joseph Roach links it to the tradition of the 'ghost-angel hybrid' (Roach, 2014: 133) – a feminized, prettified version of the spectres in revenge drama. And Evelina may also have owed something to the white-clad female ghost in Harriet Lee's play *The Mysterious Marriage* (1798), which Lee had circulated before the premiere of *The Castle Spectre* (Townshend, 2024: 232–233).

At once recycled and new, the Bleeding Nun and Evelina were later taken up by others, who altered and repurposed them yet again. The Nun was widely reproduced and reinvented in various contexts, including an independent ballad that Lewis included in *Tales of Wonder* (1801, 2: 167–172), chapbooks of varying lengths (Potter, 2018: 157), other Gothic novels (e.g., the tale of 'the Bleeding Nun of St. Catherine' in Horsley Curties' *Ancient Records; or, The Abbey of St. Oswythe* [1801]), phantasmagoria shows (Jones, 2021: 399–400), and 'a variety of dramatic adaptations', operettas, and even paper dolls (Hoeveler 2014: 186). Evelina did not have quite as active an afterlife, but she, too, migrated into other works, including chapbooks (Wilkinson, 1820) as well as William Holland's print *The castle spectre and her ernest admirer!* (1798), which shows her being inspected up close by George III's son Prince Ernest (see Figure 2).

Figure 2 William Holland, *The castle spectre and her ernest admirer!*, 1798. The Lewis Walpole Library, Yale University. https://collections.library.yale.edu/catalog/10996994. Access and usage rights: Public.[8]

As Townshend has recently argued, Lewis recognized and embraced the extensive literary borrowings that characterized Romantic-Gothic writing, adopting a 'conceptualisation of literary creativity as a process that depended upon the assemblage of other, pre-existent textual "ingredients"' (Townshend, 2024: 100–101). Kelly, too, took part in the same 'assemblage', participating in the pleasurable mix of repetition and variation that defined much Gothic and Romantic writing, while adapting shared materials to her own ends. Rather than being indications of her 'imitative' practices, then, Kelly's versions of the female spectre situate her firmly within the literary-cultural moment she shared with Lewis, while revealing much about what she found both appealing and disturbing about his work.

We first encounter a decidedly Lewis-like female ghost in *Eva*, when the first of three heroines of successive generations, all named Eva, is imprisoned by her father in a Gothic nunnery after refusing an arranged marriage. The nunnery is

---

[8] The alt text in the electronic version of this Element was taken from the Yale library catalogue, https://collections.library.yale.edu/catalog/10996994.

said to be haunted by the ghost of a certain Lady Agatha, and though Eva scoffs at these stories, she is terrified one night to see a mysterious figure 'habited in black', with a 'white transparent veil' floating around her (Kelly, 1799, 1: 160). Like the Bleeding Nun, the figure carries a lamp; like Evelina, she seems more angel than ghost, the face seen through her veil 'pale, and expressive of despair, yet touchingly delicate, and affectingly composed' (1: 160). Addressing Eva in a 'sweetly sad' voice, the figure declares: 'Fear not! ... Destined bride of Reginald Glen Bolton, fear not me, but promise to poor, murdered Agatha protection for her child!' (1: 161). Having delivered her message, the figure glides away 'with the meekness of an angel's triumph' (1: 162).

The fact that the spectral figure is embodied enough to leave behind a packet of documents hints at what the novel will later reveal: she is not a ghost but a woman in disguise. Anna Davenport has known Eva's intended husband, Sir Reginald, and his sister Agatha since they were children. When Sir Reginald, coveting his sister's inheritance, forced Agatha into a convent, Anna helped her to escape and marry the man she loved. Reginald then murdered Agatha's husband; after Agatha died, he seized her infant daughter along with her fortune. Determined to enlist the help of his intended bride and convinced that 'an appearance, supposed from the dead .. could not be denied' (Kelly, 1799, 2: 35), Anna spread the rumour that Agatha's ghost haunted the convent. Having prepared a file of documents supporting her story, she dressed 'her tall slender form in the habit of a recluse' and revealed herself to Eva in 'the solemn appearance of an unquiet spirit' (2: 35).

Strikingly, Kelly's deployment of the ghostly nun seems only nominally interested in the question of whether the supernatural is 'real' or 'explained'. The ontological and epistemological dilemma that so preoccupied other Gothic novels (including *The Monk*) is invoked here only to be dismissed, trivialized by the righteousness of the figure's request. Eva immediately embraces the cause of the 'ghost' as her own, sealing 'the unuttered, yet most awful, vow' by kissing her Bible (1: 162). Reflecting on the encounter later, she remains uncertain whether what she saw was (in a typical Gothic gesture towards *Hamlet*) 'A spirit of health, or goblin damn'd', or rather a 'corporeal sufferer' who 'chose this method to convey her mysterious pleasure' (1: 163). Yet the uncertainty proves less important than helping Agatha's orphaned daughter. Forced at last to marry Sir Reginald, Eva interrupts the wedding ceremony, invoking the 'ghost' to authorize her own boldness: 'Knowest thou no impediment, Sir Reginald...? ... My warning was too solemn to be slighted! Knowest thou no orphan wronged, no blood exclaiming, from the yawning earth, Justice for my child?' (1: 203–204). Offering the packet of documents as proof, Eva demands: '[D]eliver me the orphan of poor Agatha, restore her fortune; then will the wandering spirit be at rest – then will my vow be kept, and then, such is my father's pleasure, I am your's [*sic*]!' (1: 205). Sir Reginald complies, and Agatha's infant – whom Eva adopts, and names Eva as well – regains her rightful inheritance, growing up to become the novel's main heroine.

What Kelly seems to have noticed, based on what she revises, is the sharp discrepancy between the centrality Lewis gave to his female ghosts as spectacles and the amount of agency they possess in the plot. Having dreamed up a vivid and transgressive female power for the Bleeding Nun, Lewis then delights in neutralizing this power when the Nun is subdued by an even more potent and spectacular male agent, the Wandering Jew. As though to confirm that the Nun's power was never really her own, Agnes' attempt to empower herself by 'becoming' the Nun ends in abject failure. Agnes believes that she can harness the fear that the Nun arouses and use it to escape Lindenberg Castle: as she tells Raymond, 'I shall quit my chamber, drest in the same apparel as the Ghost is supposed to wear. Whoever meets me will be too much terrified to oppose my escape' (Lewis, 1995: 148). But when she exits the castle, Raymond has already ridden away with real Nun, and she has no choice but return inside, her costume ironically proving useful only at this point. A servant who sees her cries out and falls to his knees, and Agnes 'profit[s] by his terror' (164) – but only on her way back into imprisonment. Unable to liberate herself, she remains caught up in a kind of nightmarish narrative determinism, re-enacting the Nun's fate through her own quasi-burial beneath the Priory of St. Clair.

A similar helpless recursion characterizes Lewis' Evelina, who – dramatic entrance notwithstanding – manages only to re-enact the incident that got her killed in the first place by throwing her ghostly form before Osmond, her killer and brother-in-law, just as he intends (again) to stab her husband. As a reviewer for the *Monthly Mirror* summed up the situation, 'The mischief that is done, or prevented, would have been done or prevented without her'; but, he added, 'if we pass over the *necessity* of the *Spectre*, in this play, we must allow the effect produced by her introduction, to be stronger than any thing of the sort that has been hitherto attempted' ('The Castle Spectre', 356). In other words, if we only dispense with the desire to see Evelina achieve anything we can enjoy her real function, which is to be a source of visual pleasure for the audience – and a tribute, as well, to the ingenuity of her creator.

By making the female 'spectre' into a weapon of resistance, *Eva* thus offers not simply a variation but a meaningful revision of both *The Monk* and *The Castle Spectre*. While Kelly, too, imagines women trapped in the coercive plots men devise for them, she turns the female spectre into a way *out* of such a plot, at least for one of the novel's heroines. Anna's performance is unable to prevent the older Eva's fate as a sacrifice to her father's ambitions; between them, however, she and Eva manage to liberate Agatha's baby, the Eva of the next generation, from the nefarious plans of Sir Reginald. In Kelly's hands, then, the ghostly woman becomes not an essence but a resource – a tool used by women to help each other in the struggle for sovereignty and security. With the help of this persona, which they can assume and discard as needed, they are able to communicate with each other, join forces, share information and thus surmount the barriers placed around them by controlling, greedy men.

Kelly continues to link the female spectre to effective female agency in *Edwardina*, published in 1800 under the pseudonym of Catherine Harris. Arabella, one of the heroines of this epistolary novel, is visiting her aunt and uncle in Devonshire and becomes acquainted with the local Gothic pile, the Castle of Tregelly. After discovering that Jenny, a young woman who was seduced and abandoned by a high-born lover, has been living secretly at the castle, Arabella confronts the seducer and forces him to support Jenny and the child. A mysterious message sends her to the castle again, fearing that Jenny might be in danger. As she makes her way through the castle, she suddenly hears footsteps:

> I trembled so excessively, that throwing my robe round me, I staggered to the wall for support . . . I grew breathless with horror, when the figure of a man, hastily entering, started, as if struck with sudden dread.
>
> My robe was clear muslin; and though it perfectly concealed my features from the beholder, I could perceive and distinguish objects through its thin texture.
>
> The man gazed as if transfixed, shook in every limb, and turned his eyes fearfully round, as if in hope or expectation of some appearance more desirable than mine. He advanced a step . . . at length he spoke – 'Hell and furies! who, what art thou?'
>
> I turned full upon him, still shrouded from his knowledge; agitation, terror had given a hollow tremor to my voice, and I replied –
>
> 'Monster! what hast thou destroyed? Whom dost thou persecute? Desist – repent – repent!'
>
> 'Oh, Oh!' in lengthened agony, burst from his quivering lips. He leaned for support on his sword. (2: 93–94)

Describing the scene in retrospect, Arabella comments: 'I . . . stood in an attitude, I imagine *not unlike that of the famed Spectre of the Castle*' (2: 96, italics added). Frightened as she is at first, she quickly becomes aware that she herself is now the source of fear. Her appearance so flusters the man that he drops his sword, and Arabella picks it up and charges past him, discovering a damp dungeon where not Jenny but an old man is being held prisoner. When her pursuer threatens to shoot the old man, Arabella stabs him. The prisoner turns out to be Lord Haverland, the uncle of the eponymous heroine Edwardina and her brother Horace, Arabella's husband. He was abducted by his own son, Francis, who needed his father's money to cover his debts; by wounding Francis and setting Lord Haverland free, Arabella helps bring about the novel's happy ending.

Amplifying what she had done in *Eva*, Kelly this time embeds the borrowed figure of the 'Spectre of the Castle' in a gratifying fantasy of female heroism, which is signalled by the heroine's name. Arabella's uncle, indeed, makes the connection explicit when he mocks Arabella's efforts on behalf of Jenny: 'you are nearly as quixotical as your namesake of redoubtable memory; you are certainly run wild in romance, and will soon be armed *cap-à-pee* [sic], asserting the love rights of all the ruinated forsaken damsels in our island' (2: 82). But despite the nod to Charlotte Lennox's *The Female Quixote* (1752), nothing about Kelly's Arabella suggests a mind confused by excessive romance-reading. As soon as she lays eyes on Tregelly Castle, Arabella knows that she has come across a fictional cliché. With a maturity and self-awareness that Catherine Morland needs all of *Northanger Abbey* to develop, she mocks herself for the expectations the setting arouses in her: 'Like the heroines of romance, I expected to behold subterranean caverns, damp dungeons, confessionals, oral chambers, and a long list of *et ceteras*; but no – a few Gothic cheerless apartments, and wild, magnificent, long neglected gardens were all I could discover' (Kelly 1800, 2: 3–4).

The invocation of Lennox, then, is meant not to characterize Kelly's Arabella as deluded but rather – I would argue – to echo the longing for heroic female action that runs through *The Female Quixote* as well. As Laurie Langbauer has noted, 'The Amazons of romance come up again and again in *The Female Quixote*, and become the symbol for women's usurpation of men's power. Their repeated mention suggests that both Lennox and Arabella find them attractive and noteworthy' (47) – and so, apparently, do Kelly and *her* Arabella. The 'famed Spectre' enables Arabella to perform precisely the heroic function that her uncle mocks, an experience that leaves her exhilarated: 'Never could I have imagined that my nature possessed such energy of feeling, my mind such courage, or my arm such strength', she writes to Edwardina. 'I was not myself; my powers were not my own, and to the great Almighty be the glory ascribed' (Kelly, 1800 2: 87). Despite the requisite nod towards Providence here, we might also say that the power Arabella wields comes from assuming the 'attitude of the famed Spectre'. Instead of sinking her into Gothic delusion, her reading has given her – like Kelly – the inspiration and means to make the Gothic story her own, using its power to change reality for the better.

4.3 Coda: Kelly, Lewis and the Question of Influence

Here, in summary, is the prequel to the Kelly–Lewis story that I have tried to tell in this section, expanded somewhat with the help of the research presented throughout this Element. In 1794 Isabella Kelly began her career as a novelist for the Minerva Press. Drawing on the familiar fictional materials of the day, she started writing novels that combined Gothic and sentimental conventions, while focusing on themes of particular interest to her, such as marital difficulty and male unreliability. She clearly had her eye on successful models, as many popular novelists did, but she did not limit herself to them: her earliest fictions already show her veering away from Radcliffe's successful example to try out her own stylistic and thematic preferences.

In 1796 she read *The Monk*, in which she saw her own interests powerfully amplified. Lewis' work was inspiring, but also disquieting: she began to talk back to it in her fiction – a quiet, determined, one-sided conversation, which allowed her to sharpen her own convictions and strategies. At some point Lewis became aware of Kelly's existence, though it is not clear exactly when. It may have been after she made an explicit reference to *The Castle Spectre* in *Edwardina*, though it is also possible that Lewis was enlisted as a subscriber to *Ruthinglenne* in 1801 by Kelly's patron Lady Dalling, whom he might have known through their shared connections in Jamaica (see Shapira, 2022: 133–134). Their first documented exchange, dated August 1802, is the letter in which Lewis informs Kelly of his financial inquiries on her behalf.

My prequel now meets the published record of the story, with its two familiar figures – patron and supplicant; canonical novelist and trade novelist; author and 'drudge'. As Kelly's novels have told us, however, this version of events is only a small part of a larger picture, and one that possibly conceals more than it reveals. We have no first-hand account of how Kelly herself experienced the relationship with Lewis once he stopped being only a textual interlocutor and became her benefactor. The gratitude she expresses towards him is surely genuine: his support of William was invaluable to her, and she also benefitted from the introduction to his publisher, Bell, with whom she published *The Baron's Daughter* (1802). It must have been out of true appreciation that she sought to dedicate the novel to Lewis, which he would not allow. But knowing what we know (see Section 2.3) about her calculated use of dedications to raise her work's profile, she may have also wanted the advantage that such a public association would bring her. Did she really have nothing to do with the advertisement announcing her connection to Lewis? Lewis seems to have accepted her claims of innocence, but we have no way of confirming their veracity.

There is one other thing we do know, because Lewis mentions it in his letters: Lewis gave Kelly a 'plan of a novel', which she did not use when writing *The Baron's Daughter* (Baron Wilson 1: 279). None of Lewis' biographers have thought to wonder at this detail: why would 'poor Mrs. Kelly', desperately recycling the inventions of others for profit, refuse a ready-made outline from one of the premier Gothic writers of the day? Read in light of the discussion above, Kelly's actions become more understandable. She needed help getting William a proper education, and she was grateful for Lewis' advice and connections as she broke away from the Minerva Press. But she did not actually need Lewis' help in writing novels. His example inspired and energized her, but she had ideas of her own about Gothic storytelling. And so she ignored Lewis' 'plan of a novel' and wrote her own.

That novel, *The Baron's Daughter*, is also filled with allusions to *The Monk*, too diverse and extensive to be discussed here. It is worth noting only that its end involves the appearance of a shape-shifting female demon, who sinks 'huge and terrific claws' into the dead villain before flying away 'with something between a laugh of malice and a fearful yell' (Kelly, 1802, 4: 110). An obvious homage to the ending of *The Monk*, Kelly's demon shows that even once she knew Lewis, she was not done talking back to his writing, in particular where gender, horror and spectacle were concerned.

By way of conclusion to this section and to the Element as a whole, I want to offer one last, speculative twist to the story of Kelly and Lewis – and also, by implication, to the common story of canonical and trade Gothic. I noted (Section 4.1) certain similarities of detail between Kelly's fiery ghost scene in *The Abbey of St. Asaph* and Matilda's summoning of the demon in *The Monk*. Some other curious overlaps are worth noting here. First, consider the Gothic plotline of *The Abbey of St. Asaph*, in which a villain gains his title and estate by plotting the murder of his older brother. Although the villain believes the brother is dead, the latter has secretly been kept alive in the castle dungeon by the villain's henchman. He is discovered there by his daughter, the heiress to the estate, who was raised by poor villagers in a nearby cottage and has only recently returned to the castle, where various strange occurrences have pushed her onto a journey of discovery. This is the story of Sir Hugh, Doctor Martin, Sir Eldred and Jennet in *The Abbey of St. Asaph*, the novel Kelly published in 1795; it is also the story of Osmond, Kenrick, Reginald and Angela in *The Castle Spectre*, the play that Lewis first presented to the world in 1797. The fact that the Gothic structures in which both stories take place are set in the same location – Wales – only adds to the coincidence.

Another coincidence involves a brief scene in a novel I have not discussed here, *Joscelina, or the Rewards of Benevolence*, which Kelly published in 1797. A minor character named St. Evermond is haunted by the memory of his dead wife, who at one point returns to him in a terrifying vision: 'hark! that crack – it bursts, it yawns, it is the tomb of murdered Adela! it gasps, and now behold she rises from her earthy bed! – see she glides, she comes to blast thee, curse thee!'

(Kelly, 1798, 2: 135). A reader familiar with Lewis' work will once again suspect here the effect of his influence on Kelly: there is a strong similarity between the dream of St. Evermond – whose real name, we later learn, is *Oswald* – and that of *Osmond* in *The Castle Spectre*, whose nightmare presents to him, too, a 'female form glid[ing]' towards him among the 'tombs' (Lewis, 1798: 67). Chronological detail, however, establishes that Lewis could not have been Kelly's model. *Joscelina* was advertised as published in June of 1797 and reviewed in September and November of that year; *The Castle Spectre* did not open at Drury Lane until December, and its printed version appeared only in early 1798.

Might Lewis, then, have been reading Kelly even before *Edwardina*? Might he even have, on occasion, helped himself to a bit of inspiration from *her* – one more piece to be thrown into the mix of influences that nourished his own inventions? Beyond the tiny scraps of suggestion I've assembled here, nothing in the surviving record tells us what Lewis thought of Kelly's writing. In a later letter, apparently responding to his mother's dismissal of Kelly (by then, the remarried Mrs. Hegeland) and her circle as insufficiently genteel, Lewis refused to align himself with his mother's snobbery:

> As to what you say about Mrs. H[edgeland's] acquaintance and your own, with all that I have nothing to do: I care nothing about rank in life, nothing about what other people may think or may say.... I live as much with actors, and musicians, and painters, as with princes and politicians, and am as well satisfied, and better indeed, with the society of the first, as with that of the latter. But I absolutely require that people should possess some quality or other to amuse me or interest me, or I had rather be by myself. (Baron Wilson, 1: 362)

Did Kelly possess 'some quality to amuse... or interest' Lewis? Had he been enjoying her books before they ever met, perhaps adding them, too, to the rich reservoir on which he drew in fashioning his own creations? Even if he did, there is good reason to think he would not have felt comfortable acknowledging a literary debt to Kelly. Lewis may have liked Kelly personally; he may indeed have counted her among those whose society he enjoyed; and he may well have began to read her before becoming a published author himself, and perhaps even continued to relish her fiction and occasionally sample from it as his own career took shape. Yet given the contempt with which Minerva novels were generally regarded by the early 1800s, admitting to this influence would have been far more embarrassing for Lewis than brazenly acknowledging his debts to Shakespeare or Schiller. His bold declaration to his mother notwithstanding, egalitarianism could only go so far.

In the end, I cannot conclusively show that Lewis learned or borrowed anything from Kelly, just as it is impossible to prove that Radcliffe was responding to the trade fiction being published around her, although there is some textual evidence to suggest that she was (see Shapira, 2020a: 334–336). What I have tried to demonstrate, however, is that when we replace the cardboard cutout of the 'drudge' with a rounder authorial figure, it becomes easier to imagine that Kelly and Lewis' relationship – both personal and literary – might have been more complicated than we have always thought. If we keep exploring that possibility on a larger scale, we may also be able to tell new, more nuanced stories about the broader relations between trade fiction and the Gothic canon.

References

Alexander Heathcote Fordyce, Record of Baptism, 23 February 1763. England Births and Baptisms 1538–1975, findmypast.co.uk (accessed 23 September 2024).

Amelia Elizabeth Mary Fordice, Record of Baptism, 5 July 1768. England Births and Baptisms 1538-1975, findmypast.co.uk (accessed 23 September 2024).

Algar, Frank, *Letter to Louis F. Peck, 12 September 1955*a. Louis F. Peck Papers, bMS Eng 1260 (53), Houghton Library, Harvard University.

Algar, Frank, *Letter to Louis F. Peck, 10 October 1955*b. Louis F. Peck Papers, bMS Eng 1260 (53), Houghton Library, Harvard University.

Austen, Jane, *Northanger Abbey, Lady Susan, The Watsons, Sanditon*, edited by James Kinsley and John Davie (Oxford: Oxford University Press, 2003).

Baron Wilson, Margaret, *The Life and Correspondence of M. G. Lewis, with Many Pieces in Prose and Verse, Never before Published*, 2 vols (London: Henry Colburn, 1839).

Barthes, Roland, 'The Death of the Author', in *Image / Music / Text*, trans. Stephen Heath (London: Fontana, 1977), pp. 142–148.

Batchelor, Jennie, 'The Claims of Literature: Women Applicants to the Royal Literary Fund, 1790-1810', *Women's Writing* 12:3 (2005): 505–521.

Behrendt, Stephen C., 'Isabella Fordyce Kelly – c. 1759-1857', in Stephen C. Behrendt and Nancy Kushigian (eds.), *Scottish Women Poets of the Romantic Period* (Alexandria: Alexander Street, 2002).

Bennett, Andrew, *The Author* (Abingdon: Routledge, 2005).

Birkhead, Edith, *The Tale of Terror: A Study of the Gothic Romance* (London: Constable, 1921).

Blake, Whitney, *Letter to Louis F. Peck, 9 June 1959*. Louis F. Peck Papers, bMS Eng 1260 (53), Houghton Library, Harvard University.

Blakey, Dorothy, *The Minerva Press* (Oxford: Bibliographical Society, 1939).

Boaden, James, *Fontainville Forest; A Play, in Five Acts* (London: Printed for Hookham and Carpenter, 1794).

Boaden, James, *Memoirs of the Life of John Philip Kemble, Esq.: Including a History of the Stage, from the Time of Garrick to the Present Period*, 2 vols (London: Longman, Hurst, Rees, Orme, Brown, and Green, 1825).

Bradford, Richard, 'Literary Biography, Literary Studies, and Theory: An Uneasy Relationship', in Richard Bradford (ed.), *A Companion to Literary Biography* (Chichester: Wiley-Blackwell, 2019), pp. 339–356.

References

Brown, Susan, Patricia Clements, and Isobel Grundy (eds.), *Orlando: Women's Writing in the British Isles from the Beginnings to the Present* (Cambridge: Cambridge University Press, 2024a), https://orlando.cambridge.org/ [last accessed 11 February 2025].

Brown, Susan, Patricia Clements, and Isobel Grundy (eds.), 'Isabella Kelly Profile', in *Orlando: Women's Writing in the British Isles from the Beginnings to the Present*, (Cambridge: Cambridge University Press, 2024b), https://orlando.cambridge.org/profiles/kellis [last accessed 11 February 2025].

Burgess, Miranda, 'Secret History in the Romantic Period', in Rebecca Bullard and Rachel Carnell (eds.), *The Secret History in Literature, 1660–1820* (Cambridge: Cambridge University Press, 2017), pp. 188–201.

Campbell, Jill, '"I Am No Giant": Horace Walpole, Heterosexual Incest, and Love Among Men', *The Eighteenth Century: Theory and Interpretation* 39:3 (1998): 238–260.

Cannadine, David (ed.), *The Oxford Dictionary of National Biography* (Oxford: Oxford University Press, 2004), www.oxforddnb.com [last accessed 22 March 2025].

'The Castle Spectre. Written by M.G. Lewis, Esq., M.P.', *Monthly Mirror* 4 (1797): 354–356.

Chaplin, Sue, 'Ann Radcliffe and Romantic-Era Fiction', in Dale Townshend and Angela Wright (eds.), *Ann Radcliffe, Romanticism and the Gothic* (Cambridge: Cambridge University Press, 2014), pp. 203–218.

Clery, E. J., *The Rise of Supernatural Fiction, 1762–1800* (Cambridge: Cambridge University Press, 1995).

Coleridge, Samuel Taylor, 'The Monk: A Romance', *The Critical Review; or, Annals of Literature* 19 (February 1797): 194–200.

Copeland, Edward, *Women Writing about Money: Women's Fiction in England, 1790–1820* (Cambridge: Cambridge University Press, 1995).

Cox, Jeffrey N., 'Introduction: Reanimating Gothic Drama', *Gothic Studies* 3:2 (2001): 107–116.

Cross, Nigel, *The Common Writer: Life in Nineteenth Century Grub Street* (Cambridge: Cambridge University Press, 1988).

Czlapinski, Rebecca and Eric C. Wheeler, 'The Real Eleanor Sleath', *Studies in Gothic Fiction* 2:1 (2011): 5–12.

Davies, Colette, 'Women Writers, Authorship, and the Late-Eighteenth Century Novel: Representations of the Female Author in the Minerva Press (1785–1800)', Ph.D. dissertation, University of Nottingham, 2022.

DeLucia, JoEllen, 'Radcliffe Incorporated: Ann Radcliffe, Mary Ann Radcliffe and the Minerva Author', *Romantic Textualities: Literature and Print*

Culture, 1780–1840 23 (2020), https://romtext.cardiffuniversitypress.org/articles/10.18573/romtext.74 [last accessed 2 June 2025].

Duncker, Patricia, 'Mary Shelley's Afterlives: Biography and Invention', *Women: A Cultural Review* 15:2 (2004): 230–249.

'Education', *The British Review, and London Critical Journal*, 23 vols., (London: Longman, Hurst, Rees, Orme, and Brown, 1811), 1: 511.

Ellis, Kate Ferguson. *The Contested Castle: Gothic Novels and the Subversion of Domestic Ideology* (Urbana: University of Illinois Press, 1989).

Evans, Bertram, *Gothic Drama from Walpole to Shelley* (Berkeley: University of California Press, 2020).

Ferris, Ina, *The Achievement of Literary Authority: Gender, History, and the Waverly Novels* (Ithaca: Cornell University Press, 1991).

Fishelov, David, 'Types of Characters, Characteristics of Types', *Style* 24:3 (1990): 422–439.

Forster, E. M., *Aspects of the Novel* (London: Edward Arnold, 1927).

Foucault, Michel, 'What Is an Author?', in Donald F. Bouchard (ed.), *Language, Counter-Memory, Practice: Selected Essays and Interviews*, trans. Donald F. Bouchard and Sherry Sim (Ithaca: Cornell University Press, 1977), pp. 113–138.

Frank, Frederick S., *The First Gothics: A Critical Guide to the English Gothic Novel* (New York: Garland, 1987).

Gamer, Michael, 'Assimilating the Novel: Reviews and Collections,' in Peter Garside and Karen O'Brien (eds.), *The Oxford History of the Novel in English, Vol. 2: English and British Fiction 1750–1820* (Oxford: Oxford University Press, 2015), pp. 531–549.

Garside, Peter, James Raven and Rainer Schöwerling, *The English Novel 1770–1829: A Bibliographical Survey of Prose Fiction Published in the British Isles*, 2 vols (Oxford: Oxford University Press, 2000).

Greene, Richard, 'Kelly [née Fordyce; Other Married Name Hedgeland], Isabella (bap. 1759, d. 1857), Poet and Novelist', revised by Pam Perkins, *Oxford Dictionary of National Biography*, 23 September 2004, www.oxforddnb.com/view/10.1093/ref:odnb/9780198614128.001.0001/odnb-9780198614128-e-37626 [last accessed 5 October 2023].

Haggerty, George, 'Literature and Homosexuality in the Late Eighteenth Century: Walpole, Beckford, and Lewis', *Studies in the Novel* 18:4 (1986): 341–352.

Hoeveler, Diane Long, 'Charlotte Dacre's Zofloya: The Gothic Demonization of the Jew', in Sheila A. Spector (ed.), *The Jews and British Romanticism: Politics, Religion, Culture* (New York: Palgrave Macmillan, 1995), pp. 165–178.

Hoeveler, Diane Long, 'Gothic Adaptation, 1764–1830', in Glennis Byron and Dale Townshend (eds.), *The Gothic World* (London: Routledge, 2014), pp. 185–198.

Horsley Curties, T. J., *Ancient Records, or, the Abbey of St. Oswythe, a Romance*, 4 vols (London: William Lane, 1801).

Hudson, Hannah Doherty, 'The Myth of Minerva: Publishing, Popular Fiction, and the Rise of the Novel', Ph.D. dissertation, Stanford University, 2013.

Hudson, Hannah Doherty, 'Imitation, Intertextuality and the Minerva Press Novel,' *Romantic Textualities* 23 (2020): 149–167, www.romtext.org.uk/articles/rt23_n09/ [last accessed 1 June 2024].

Hudson, Hannah Doherty, *Romantic Fiction and Literary Excess in the Minerva Press Era* (Cambridge: Cambridge University Press, 2023).

Hudson, Kathleen (ed.), *Women's Authorship and the Early Gothic: Legacies and Innovations* (Cardiff: University of Wales Press, 2020).

Jacobs, Edward D., *Accidental Migrations: An Archaeology of Gothic Discourse* (Lewisburg: Bucknell University Press, 2000).

Jerdan, William, *The Autobiography of William Jerdan... with His Literary, Political, and Social Reminiscences and Correspondence During the Last Fifty Years*, 4 vols (London: Arthur Hall, Virtue, 1852–1853).

Jerdan, William, 'Characteristic Letters: Communicated by the Author of "Men I Have Known"', *The Leisure Hour: A Family Journal of Instruction and Recreation*, 4 December 1869, pp. 781–783.

Johnson, Claudia, L., *Equivocal Beings: Politics, Gender and Sentimentality in the 1790s: Wollstonecraft, Radcliffe, Burney, Austen* (Chicago: University of Chicago Press, 1995).

Johnson, Claudia L., 'The Divine Miss Jane: Jane Austen, Janeites, and the Discipline of Novel Studies', *Boundary* 2:23 (1996): 143–163.

Jones, David Annwn, 'The Art of Ghostly Projections', in Clive Bloom (ed.), *The Palgrave Handbook of Gothic Origins* (Cham: Palgrave Macmillan, 2021), pp. 397–406.

Joseph Hedgeland, Record of Burial, 24 January 1812. Church of England Baptisms, Marriages and Burials 1538–1812, ancestry.co.uk [accessed 9 September 2023].

Joseph Hedgeland and *Isabella Kelly, Record of Marriage, 22 May 1809*. Reference number P74/Luk/202, London Metropolitan Archives, ancestry.com [accessed 24 September 2024].

Kelly, Isabella, *A Collection of Poems and Fables* (London: Printed for the author, 1794a).

Kelly, Isabella, *Madeline, or the Castle of Montgomery*, 3 vols (London: William Lane, 1794b).

Kelly, Isabella, *Letter to Warren Hastings, 31 May 1795*a. Add MS 29174: April 1795–December 1796, Vol. 43 of The Official and Private Correspondence of Warren Hastings, Governor General of India. British Library.

Kelly, Isabella, *The Abbey of St. Asaph*, 3 vols (London: William Lane, 1795b).

Kelly, Isabella, *The Ruins of Avondale Priory*, 3 vols (London: William Lane, 1796).

Kelly, Isabella, *Joscelina: or, the Rewards of Benevolence*, 2nd ed., 2 vols (London: William Lane, 1798).

Kelly, Isabella, *Eva, A Novel*, 3 vols (London: William Lane, 1799).

Kelly, Isabella [as Catherine Harris], *Edwardina*, 2 vols (London: William Lane, 1800).

Kelly, Isabella, *Ruthinglenne; or, the Critical Moment*, 3 vols (London: T.N. Longman and O. Rees, 1801).

Kelly, Isabella, *The Baron's Daughter: A Novel*, 4 vols (London: J. Bell, 1802).

Kelly, Isabella, *A Modern Incident in Domestic Life*, 2 vols (Brentford: P. Norbury, 1803).

Kelly, Isabella, *The Secret*, 4 vols (Brentford: P. Norbury, 1805a).

Kelly, Isabella, *The Child's French Grammar* (Brentford: P. Norbury, 1805b).

Kelly, Isabella, *Poems and Fables on Several Occasions* (Chelsea: Stanhope and Tilling, 1807).

Kelly, Isabella, *Literary Information; Consisting of Anecdotes, Explanations, and Derivations* (1811).

Kelly, Isabella, *Jane De Dunstanville*, 4 vols (London: J. Souter, 1813).

Kelly, Isabella, *Instructive Anecdotes for Youth* (London: Printed for Weed and Rider, 1819).

Kelly, Isabella, *Memoir of the Late Mrs. Henrietta Fordyce* [...] (London: Printed for Hurst, Robinson, 1823).

Kelly, Isabella [as Isabella Hedgeland], *Letter to W. T. Fitzgerald, 21 July 1828*a. Loan 96 RLF 1/632/3, Archive of the Royal Literary Fund (1790-1990s), British Library.

Kelly, Isabella [as Isabella Hedgeland], *Letter to W. T. Fitzgerald, 25 July 1828*b. Loan 96 RLF 1/632/2, Archive of the Royal Literary Fund (1790–1990s), British Library.

Kelly, Isabella [as Isabella Hedgeland], *Letter to Joseph Snow, 25 October 1832*. Loan 96 RLF 1/632/12, Archive of the Royal Literary Fund (1790–1990s), British Library.

Kelly, Isabella, *ProQuest Biographies* (Ann Arbor: ProQuest, 2015), Literature Online Database [last accessed September 7, 2023].

Kelly, Robert, Col., *Letter to Brigadier General Giles Stibbert, 8 November 1781*. IOR/P/2/47 fols. 412-413, Bengal Proceedings (15 October 1781–24 December 1781), British Library.

Kelly, Robert, Col., *Letter to Executor and Amended Will, 25 July 1790*. IOR/L/AG/34/29/193, fols. 16–19, Madras Wills and Administrations, British Library.

Kelly, Robert Hawke, *Petition to the Chairman and Directors of the East India Company, Read January 30, 1793*. IOR/E/1/89, Miscellaneous Letters Received (1793), East India Company General Correspondence, British Library.

Langbauer, Laurie, 'Romance Revised: Charlotte Lennox's *The Female Quixote*', *Novel: A Forum on Fiction* 18:1(1984): 29–49.

Lanser, Susan S., 'The Author's Queer Clothes: Anonymity, Sex(uality), and *the Travels and Adventures of Mademoiselle de Richelieu*', in Robert J. Griffin (ed.), *The Faces of Anonymity: Anonymous and Pseudonymous Publication from the Sixteenth to the Twentieth Century* (New York: Palgrave Macmillan, 2003), pp. 81–102.

Lewis, Matthew Gregory, *The Castle Spectre* (London: J. Bell, 1798).

Lewis, Matthew Gregory, *The Monk*, ed. Howard Anderson (Oxford: Oxford World Classics, 1995).

Lloyd, Nicola, 'The Fiction of Mary Julia Young: Female Trade Gothic and Romantic Genre-Mixing', in Kathleen Hudson (ed.), *Women's Authorship and the Early Gothic: Legacies and Innovations* (Cardiff: University of Wales Press, 2020), pp. 133–155.

Lonsdale, Roger (ed.), *Eighteenth Century Women Poets: An Oxford Anthology* (Oxford: Oxford University Press, 1989).

Looser, Devoney, *Sister Novelists: The Trailblazing Porter Sisters, Who Paved the Way for Austen and the Brontës* (London: Bloomsbury, 2022).

Macdonald, D. L., *Monk Lewis: A Critical Biography* (Toronto: University of Toronto Press, 2000).

Macdonald, Simon, 'Identifying Mrs Meeke: Another Burney Family Novelist', *The Review of English Studies* 64:265 (2013): 367–385.

Mackley, J. S., 'The Re-Discovery of Eleanor Sleath', in Clive Bloom (ed.), *The Palgrave Handbook of Gothic Origins* (Cham: Palgrave, 2021), pp. 177–195.

Mandal, Anthony, 'Gothic and the Publishing World, 1780–1820', in Glennis Byron and Dale Townshend (eds.), *The Gothic World* (London: Routledge, 2014), pp. 159–171.

Mandal, Anthony, 'Fiction', in Devoney Looser (ed.), *The Cambridge Companion to Women's Writing in the Romantic Period* (Cambridge: Cambridge University Press, 2015), pp. 16–31.

Mandal, Anthony, 'Mrs. Meeke and Minerva: The Mystery of the Marketplace', *Eighteenth-Century Life* 42.2 (2018): 131–151.

Margaret Jemima Fordice, Record of Baptism, 9 October 1760. England Births and Baptisms 1538–1975, findmypast.co.uk (accessed 23 September 2024).

Mason, Nicholas, *Literary Advertising and the Shaping of British Romanticism* (Johns Hopkins University Press, 2013).

McLeod, Deborah Anne, 'The Minerva Press', Ph.D. dissertation (University of Alberta, 1997).

Mellor, Anne K., *Mary Shelley: Her Life, Her Fiction, Her Monsters* (London: Routledge, 2012).

Milbank, Alison, 'Bleeding Nuns: A Genealogy of the Female Gothic Grotesque,' in Diana Wallace and Andrew Smith (eds.), *The Female Gothic: New Directions* (London: Palgrave Macmillan, 2009), pp. 76–97.

Miles, Robert, *Ann Radcliffe: The Great Enchantress* (Manchester: Manchester University Press, 1995).

Miles, Robert, '"Mother Radcliff": Ann Radcliffe and the Female Gothic', in Diana Wallace and Andrew Smith (eds.), *The Female Gothic: New Directions* (London: Palgrave Macmillan, 2009), pp. 42–59.

Miles, Robert, 'Ann Radcliffe and Matthew Lewis', in David Punter (ed.), *A New Companion to the Gothic* (Malden: Wiley-Blackwell, 2012), pp. 91–109.

Moers, Ellen, *Literary Women* (London: Women's Press, 1978).

Morin, Christina, *Charles Robert Maturin and the Haunting of Irish Romantic Fiction* (Manchester: Manchester University Press, 2011).

Morin, Christina, *The Gothic Novel in Ireland, c. 1760–1829* (Manchester: Manchester University Press, 2018).

Morris, Marilyn, 'The Royal Family and Family Values in Late Eighteenth-Century England', *Journal of Family History* 21:4 (October 1996): 519–532.

Morton, Karen, *A Life Marketed as Fiction: An Analysis of the Works of Eliza Parsons* (Kansas City: Valancourt Books, 2011).

'The Mother of Sir Fitzroy Kelly' (1848), Loan 96 RLF 1/632/14, Archive of the Royal Literary Fund (1790–1990s), British Library.

Mowl, Timothy, *Horace Walpole: The Great Outsider* (London: Faber & Faber, 2014).

Neiman, Elizabeth, *Minerva's Gothics: The Politics and Poetics of Romantic Exchange, 1780–1820* (Cardiff: University of Wales Press, 2019).

Neiman, Elizabeth, and Christina Morin (eds.), *The Minerva Press and the Literary Marketplace*, Special Issue of *Romantic Textualities: Literature and Print Culture, 1780–1840* 23 (2020), https://romtext.cardiffuniversitypress.org/4/volume/0/issue/23.

Nicholls, C. S., and G. H. L. LeMay, *Dictionary of National Biography: Missing Persons* (Oxford: Oxford University Press, 1993).

Nixon, Cheryl L., 'Ann Radcliffe's Commonplace Book: Assembling the Female Body and the Material Text', *Women's Writing* 22:3 (2015): 355–375.

Norton, Rictor, *Mistress of Udolpho: The Life of Ann Radcliffe* (London: Leicester University Press, 1999).

'Novels and Romances', *The Critical Review* 14 (July 1795): 349–356.

O'Connell, Lisa, *The Origins of the English Marriage Plot: Literature, Politics and Religion in the Eighteenth Century* (Cambridge: Cambridge University Press, 2019).

Owen Charles Fordice, Record of Baptism, 5 January 1767. Scotland, Parish Births and Baptisms 1564–1929, findmypast.co.uk [accessed 24 September 2024].

Peck, Louis F., *Letter to Frank Algar, 9 September 1955*a. Louis F. Peck Papers, bMS Eng 1260 (52). Houghton Library, Harvard University.

Peck, Louis F., *Letter to Frank Algar, 28 October 1955*b. Louis F. Peck Papers, bMS Eng 1260 (52), Houghton Library, Harvard University.

Peck, Louis F., *A Life of Matthew G. Lewis* (Cambridge, MA: Harvard University Press, 1961).

Peiser, Megan, 'William Lane and the Minerva Press in the Review Periodical, 1790–1820', *Romantic Textualities: Literature and Print Culture, 1780–1840* 23 (Summer 2020): 124–148, www.romtext.org.uk/articles/rt23_n08/ [last accessed 28 February 2024].

Phillimore, R. H., *Historical Records of the Survey of India*, 4 vols (Dehra Dun: Surveyor General of India, 1946–1958).

Potter, Franz J., *The History of Gothic Publishing, 1800–1835: Exhuming the Trade* (Basingstoke: Palgrave Macmillan, 2005).

Potter, Franz J., 'Horror in Gothic Chapbooks', in Kevin Corstorphine and Laura R. Kremmel (eds.), *The Palgrave Handbook to Horror Literature* (Cham: Palgrave Macmillan, 2018), pp. 155–163.

Punter, David, *The Literature of Terror: A History of Gothic Fictions from 1765 to the Present Day*, 2nd ed., 2 vols (London: Longman, 1996).

Punter, David and Alan Bissett, 'Francis Lathom in the Eighteenth Century', *Gothic Studies* 5:1 (2003): 55–70.

Radcliffe, Ann, *The Mysteries of Udolpho*, ed. Bonamy Dobrée (Oxford: Oxford World's Classics, 1998).

Raisanen, Elizabeth, 'Kelly (née Fordyce), Isabella', in Natasha Duquette (ed.), *The Palgrave Encyclopedia of Romantic-Era Women's Writing* (Cham: Palgrave Macmillan, 2020; entry updated 2024), pp. 1–5.

Roach, Joseph, '"Pretty Ghost, a Duet": On Dying While You Still Look Good', in Mary Luckhurst and Emilie Morin (eds.), *Theatre and Ghosts: Materiality, Performance and Modernity* (London: Palgrave Macmillan UK, 2014), pp. 128–140.

Robert Kelly and Isabella Fordice, Record of Marriage, 14 November 1789. Reference number MS10091/161, London and Surrey, England, Marriage Bonds and Allegations, 1597–1921, www.ancestry.co.uk [accessed 10 September 2023].

Roche, Regina Maria, *Letter to the Royal Literary Fund, 30 April 1830.* Archives of the Royal Literary Fund, World Microfilms, *Nineteenth Century Collections Online* [last accessed 7 January 2025].

Rossetti, Christina, *Letter to the Editor of the Athanæum, 2 July 1883.* Letter 1137 in The Letters of Christina Rossetti, University of Virginia Press, https://rotunda.upress.virginia.edu/crossetti/default.xqy [accessed 23 January 2024].

Sangster, Matthew, *Living as an Author in the Romantic Period* (Cham: Palgrave Macmillan, 2021).

Scott, Walter, 'Prefatory Memoir to Mrs. Ann Radcliffe', in *The Novels of Mrs. Ann Radcliffe [...] to Which Is Prefixed, a Memoir of the Life of the Author* (London: Hurst, Robinson, 1824), pp. i–xxxix.

Seymour, Miranda, *Mary Shelley* (London: Faber & Faber, 2011).

Shapira, Yael, 'Beyond the Radcliffe "Formula": Isabella Kelly and the Gothic Troubles of the Married Heroine', *Women's Writing* 26.3 (2015): 245–263. https://doi.org/10.1080/09699082.2015.1110289.

Shapira, Yael, 'Gothic Fiction beyond Radcliffe and Lewis', in Dale Townshend and Angela Wright (eds.), *The Cambridge History of the Gothic, Volume 1: Gothic in the Long Eighteenth Century* (Cambridge: Cambridge University Press, 2020a), pp. 323–344.

Shapira, Yael, 'Isabella Kelly and the Minerva Gothic Challenge', *Romantic Textualities: Literature and Print Culture, 1780–1840* 23 (2020b): 168–184, www.romtext.org.uk/articles/rt23_n10/ [accessed 4 February 2025].

Shapira, Yael, 'What "Poor Mrs. Kelly" Saw: Isabella Kelly Reads *The Monk*', in Kathleen Hudson (ed.), *Women's Authorship and the Early Gothic: Legacies and Innovations* (Cardiff: University of Wales Press, 2020c), pp. 78–81.

Shapira, Yael. 'Somebody's Complaint: Isabella Kelly, Warren Hastings, and the Strange Case of Ruthinglenne', *Eighteenth-Century Life* 46.2 (2022): 113–142.

St. Clair, William, 'The Biographer as Archaeologist', in Peter France and William St. Clair (eds.), *Mapping Lives: The Uses of Biography* (Oxford: Oxford University Press, 2004), pp. 219–234.

Stanton, Judith, 'Charlotte Smith and "Mr Monstroso": An Eighteenth-Century Marriage in Life and Fiction', *Women's Writing* 7:1 (2000): 7–22.

Stephen, Leslie and Sidney Lee (eds.), *Dictionary of National Biography*, 63 vols (London: Smith, Elder, 1885–1900).

Summers, Montague, *The Gothic Quest: A History of the Gothic Novel* (New York: Russell & Russell, 1964).

Sutton, Hedley, 'Babes in Arms', *Untold Lives Blog*, British Library, 13 August 2013, https://blogs.bl.uk/untoldlives/2013/08/babes-in-arms.html [last accessed September 12, 2023].

Talfourd, Thomas Noon, 'Memoirs of the Life and Writings of Mrs. Radcliffe', in Ann Radcliffe, *Gaston de Blondeville; or, the Court of Henry III*, 4 vols (London: H. Colbourn, 1826), vol. 1, pp. 3–132.

Thomas Fordyce, Record of Baptism, 7 January 1753. OPR 168A/8, Scotland, Parish Births and Baptisms 1564–1929, findmypast.co.uk [accessed 24 September 2024].

Todd, Janet (ed.), *A Dictionary of British and American Women Writers 1660–1800* (Totowa: Rowman and Allanheld, 1985).

Townshend, Dale, 'TJ Horsley Curties and Royalist Gothic: The Case of *The Monk of Udolpho* (1807)', *Irish Journal of Gothic and Horror Studies* 4 (2008): 3–14.

Townshend, Dale, *Gothic Antiquity: History, Romance, and the Architectural Imagination, 1760–1840* (Oxford: Oxford University Press, 2019).

Townshend, Dale, *Matthew Gregory Lewis: The Gothic and Romantic Literary Culture* (Cardiff: Wales University Press, 2024).

Varma, Devendra P., *The Gothic Flame: Being a History of the Gothic Novel in England* (New York: Russell & Russell, 1966).

Watt, James, *Contesting the Gothic: Fiction, Genre and Cultural Conflict, 1764–1832* (Cambridge: Cambridge University Press, 1999).

William Robert Fordice, Record of Baptism, 14 December 1761. England Births and Baptisms 1538–1975, findmypast.co.uk [accessed 24 September 2024].

Williams, Anne, 'Reading Walpole Reading Shakespeare', in Christy Desmet and Anne Williams (eds.), *Shakespearean Gothic* (Cardiff: University of Wales Press, 2009), pp. 13–36.

Wilkinson, Sarah, *The Castle Spectre; an Ancient Baronial Romance, by S. Wilkinson, Founded on the Original Drama of M. G. L.* (London: Printed by J. Bailey, 1820).

Wimsatt Jr., W. K. and M. C. Beardsley, 'The Intentional Fallacy', *The Sewanee Review* 54:3 (1946): 468–488.

Wright, Angela, 'Scottish Gothic', in Catherine Spooner and Emma McEvoy (eds.), *The Routledge Companion to the Gothic* (London: Routledge, 2007), pp. 73–82.

Wright, Angela, 'Disturbing the Female Gothic: An Excavation of the *Northanger* Novels', in Diana Wallace and Andrew Smith (eds.), *The Female Gothic: New Directions* (London: Palgrave Macmillan, 2009), pp. 60–75.

Wymes Fordice, Record of Baptism, 2 March 1765. Scotland, Parish Births and Baptisms 1564–1929, findmypast.co.uk [accessed 24 September 2024].

Acknowledgements

This research was supported by the Israel Science Foundation (grant no. 814/23).

Cambridge Elements

The Gothic

Dale Townshend
Manchester Metropolitan University
Dale Townshend is Professor of Gothic Literature in the Manchester Centre for Gothic Studies, Manchester Metropolitan University.

Angela Wright
University of Sheffield
Angela Wright is Professor of Romantic Literature in the School of English at the University of Sheffield and co-director of its Centre for the History of the Gothic.

Advisory Board
Enrique Ajuria Ibarra, *Universidad de las Américas, Puebla, Mexico*
Xavier Aldana Reyes, *Manchester Metropolitan University, UK*
Katarzyna Ancuta, *Chulalongkorn University, Thailand*
Carol Margaret Davison, *University of Windsor, Ontario, Canada*
Rebecca Duncan, *Linnaeus University, Sweden*
Jerrold E. Hogle, *Emeritus, University of Arizona*
Mark Jancovich, *University of East Anglia, UK*
Dawn Keetley, *Lehigh University, USA*
Roger Luckhurst, *Birkbeck College, University of London, UK*
Emma McEvoy, *University of Westminster, UK*
Eric Parisot, *Flinders University, Australia*
Andrew Smith, *University of Sheffield, UK*

About the Series
Seeking to publish short, research-led yet accessible studies of the foundational 'elements' within Gothic Studies as well as showcasing new and emergent lines of scholarly enquiry, this innovative series brings to a range of specialist and non-specialist readers some of the most exciting developments in recent Gothic scholarship.

Cambridge Elements

The Gothic

Elements in the Series

Gothic Voices: The Vococentric Soundworld of Gothic Writing: Impossible Voices
Matt Foley

Mary Robinson and the Gothic
Jerrold E. Hogle

Folk Gothic
Dawn Keetley

The Last Man and Gothic Sympathy
Michael Cameron

Democracy and the American Gothic
Michael J. Blouin

Dickens and the Gothic
Andrew Smith

Contemporary Body Horror
Xavier Aldana Reyes

The Music of the Gothic 1789–1820
Emma McEvoy

The Eternal Wanderer
Mary Going

African American Gothic in the Era of Black Lives Matter
Maisha Wester

Biography and the Trade-Gothic Author: The Case of Isabella Kelly
Yael Shapira

A full series listing is available at: www.cambridge.org/GOTH

Printed by Integrated Books International,
United States of America